GW00457635

LAA

Love Addicts Anonymous

Copyright © 2023

Susan Peabody

Love Addicts Anonymous

Brighter Tomorrow Publishing

Feel free to translate this book into another language.

Contents

History of LAA

Love Adddicts Anonymous was co-founded by
Susan Peabody and Howard Gold in 2004. Prior to
this it was a "Women Who Love Too Much"
meeting which Susan founded in 1984. The name
change, in 2004, was made so that men could attend
meetings.

The purpose for the new LAA organization was for
love addicts to have their own 12-Step program
with the focus on the various types of love
addiction and codependency. Howard and Susan,
along with the first 12 members, wanted to do
something different, so it was decided to allow
"outside literature," and have a recovery reading at
the beginning of each meeting and make that the
topic and expedite recovery.

In 2004 Susan wrote the literature behind the
scenes, and Howard took on the responsibility of
facilitating the meetings starting on September 12.
The group met in Piedmont, California. About 12
people attended.

In 2014, LAA became international.

In 2019, the International Business Committee was
formed to try to bring all the meetings together to
make decisions.

In 2019 the South Africa LAA group created the logo.

On May 1, 2020, LAA was re-born under the dark cloud of Covid-19. Since then, it has grown significantly and currently has 21 meetings including the One Day at a Time Fellowship of LAA.

Today, Howard has passed on, but as of 2022 Susan still writes about recovery.

Preamble

Love Addicts Anonymous is a fellowship of men and women whose common purpose is to recover from our unhealthy dependency on love as it plays out in our fantasies and relationships. The only requirement for membership in LAA is a desire to work toward recovery. There are no dues or fees; we are self- supporting through our own contributions. Our primary purpose is to offer a safe place to recover from love addiction and to carry the message of recovery to those who still suffer.

Statement of Purpose

Love Addicts Anonymous was started to provide a safe place where love addicts could come together and recover from love addiction. While sex may play a role in our love addiction, we are not addicted to sex. We believe that love addiction is to sex addiction what drugs are to alcohol. They are alike in many ways, but they are also different, and they each deserve their own recovery program. In LAA we will share our experience, strength and hope with each other. As a group, we will support each other unconditionally. We will also read literature, share ideas, process information and work the 12-steps of LAA as adapted from Alcoholics Anonymous. Please be assured that no particular ideology will be forced upon you. You can take what you need and leave the rest. If you are a love addict, or think you might be, join us on our journey toward putting love into perspective and establishing healthy relationships with ourselves and others. Let us do together what we cannot do alone.

Welcome

Love addiction comes in many forms. Some love addicts carry a torch for unavailable people. Some love addicts obsess when they fall in love. Some love addicts get addicted to the euphoric effects of romance. Others cannot let go of a toxic relationship even if they are unhappy, depressed, lonely, neglected or in danger. Some love addicts are codependent and others are narcissistic. Some love addicts use sex to manage feelings; others are sexually anorexic. What we all have in common is that we are powerless over our distorted thoughts, feelings and behavior when it comes to love, fantasies, and relationships. Still, there is hope. Through self-honesty, open-mindedness, willingness and the 12-steps of LAA, we *can* recover. We *can* grow and change in the sunlight of the spirit. Welcome to LAA! Welcome home!

Typical Kinds of Love Addicts

I n the last decade, a lot has changed in the world of love addiction. Not that love addiction itself has changed. It is pretty much the same insidious disorder it always has been. What has changed is how the world looks at it. Twenty years ago, our understanding of love addiction was still emerging out of our understanding of codependency. Therefore, love addiction and codependency seemed to be one in the same. However, today we understand that this is not true. Love addiction stands alone, and codependency is only one of several underlying personality disorders. To make it perfectly clear how one love addict differs from another LAA has prepared the following list:

Obsessed Love Addicts (OLAs) cannot let go, even if their partners are:

- Unavailable emotionally or sexually
- Afraid to commit
- Cannot communicate
- Unloving or distant
- Abusive
- Controlling and dictatorial
- Ego-centric
- Selfish
- Addicted to something outside the relationship (hobbies, drugs, alcohol, sex)

Codependent Love Addicts (CLAs) are the most widely recognized. They fit a pretty standard profile. Most of them suffer from low self-esteem and have a certain predictable way of thinking, feeling and behaving. This means that from a place of insecurity and low self-esteem, they try desperately to hold on to the people they are addicted to using codependent behavior. This includes enabling, rescuing, caretaking, passive-aggressive controlling, and accepting neglect or abuse. In general, CLAs will do anything to "take care" of their partners in the hope that they will not leave—or that someday they will reciprocate.

Relationship Addicts (RAs), unlike other love addicts, are no longer in love with their partners but they cannot let go. Usually, they are so unhappy that the relationship is affecting their health, spirit and emotional well being. Even if their partner batters them, and they are in danger, they cannot let go. They are afraid of being alone. They are afraid of change. They do not want to hurt or abandon their partners. This can be described as "I hate you; don't leave me."

Narcissistic Love Addicts (NLAs) use dominance, seduction and withholding to control their partners. Unlike codependents, who accept a lot of discomfort, narcissists won't put up with anything that interferes with their happiness. They are self-absorbed and their low self-esteem is masked by their grandiosity. Furthermore, rather than seeming to obsess about the relationship, NLAs appear aloof and unconcerned. They do not appear to be addicted at all. Rarely do you even know that NLAs are hooked until you try to leave them. Then they will no longer be aloof and uncaring. They will panic and use anything at their disposal to hold on to the relationship—including violence. Many professionals have rejected the idea that narcissists can be love addicts. This may be because they rarely come in for treatment. However, if you have ever seen how some narcissists react to perceived or real abandonment, you will see that they are indeed "hooked."

Ambivalent Love Addicts

ALAs suffer from avoidant personality disorder—or what SLAA calls emotional anorexia. They don't have a hard time letting go, they have a hard time moving forward. They desperately crave love, but at the same time they are terrified of intimacy. This combination is agonizing. ALAs come in different forms too.

Torch Bearers obsess about someone who is unavailable. This can be done without acting out (suffering in silence) or by pursuing the person they are in love with. Some torch bearers are more addicted than others. This kind of addiction feeds on fantasies and illusions.

Saboteurs destroy relationships when they start to get serious or at whatever point their fear of intimacy comes up. This can be anytime—before the first date, after the first date, after sex, after the subject of commitment comes up—whenever.

Seductive Withholders always come on to you when they want sex or companionship. When they become frightened or feel unsafe, they begin withholding companionship, sex, affection—anything that makes them feel anxious. If they leave the relationship when they become frightened, they are just Saboteurs. If they keep repeating the pattern of being available/unavailable, they are seductive withholders.

Romance Addicts are addicted to multiple partners. Unlike sex addicts, who are trying to avoid bonding altogether, romance addicts bond with each of their partners, to one degree or another, even if the romantic liaisons are short-lived or happening simultaneously. By "romance" we mean sexual passion and pseudo emotional intimacy. Please note that while romance addicts bond with each of their partners to a degree, their goal (besides getting high off of romance and drama) is to avoid commitment or bonding on a deeper level with one partner. Often romance addicts are confused with sex addicts.

A Note about ALAs

Not all avoidants are love addicts. If you accept your fear of intimacy and social situations, and do not get hooked on unavailable people, or just keep your social circle small and unthreatening you are not necessarily an ALA. But if you eat your heart out over some unavailable person year after year, or sabotage one relationship after another, or have serial romantic affairs, or only feel close when you are with another avoidant, you may be an Ambivalent Love Addict.

Combinations

You may find that you have more than one type of love addiction. Many of these types overlap and combine themselves with other behavioral problems. For instance, you may be a codependent, alcoholic love addict. Or a love/relationship addict. The important thing is to identify your own profile so you know what you are dealing with.

Robert was a love addict, relationship addict, romance addict and sex addict. He was married but did not want to divorce his wife of twenty years even though he was not in love with her (relationship addiction) His hobby was masturbating to pornography when his wife was not home (sex addiction). He had affairs with several other women simultaneously without his wife finding out. He really cared about each of these women (romance addict). One day he met Jennifer and fell in love with her. It did not take long before he was obsessed with her. She did not want to be with him because he was married, so he began stalking and harassing her (love addict). Robert finally got into recovery, divorced his wife, gave up the pornography and affairs and married the woman he was obsessed with. At first his jealousy was out of control, but after a few years of therapy and 12-Step meetings he began to trust his new wife. Because she was mature, well-grounded and had high self esteem, the relationship began to normalize. Today, all of Robert's addictions are in remission.

Narcissists and Codependents

It is very common for love addicts to end up in relationships with other love addicts. The most common kind of love-addicted couple is, as you might have guessed, the codependent and the narcissist. In the beginning, narcissists are often seductive. After they have hooked their codependent partners, however, they change. Here is an example of a narcissist/codependent relationship.

Nancy and James met at a bar and were instantly attracted to one another. Within days, Nancy (the codependent) had fallen madly in love with James (the narcissist). From the beginning, she was helpful, nurturing, attentive and went out of her way to make him happy. James, on the other hand, appeared to be able to take or leave the relationship after they made love. He canceled dates, neglected to return phone calls, saw other women, became very domineering and for the most part seemed aloof and detached. Still, six months later, Nancy married James because she was in love with him and secretly hoped that he would change.

After Nancy and James were married, the pattern of neglect continued—especially his affairs with other women. When Nancy objected, James bullied her until she stopped nagging him about it. This went on for years. Nancy tried to save her marriage by placating James in every way she could think of, but he continued to do what he wanted. Eventually, Nancy stopped loving James and thought about leaving him, but she just couldn't bring herself to face the loneliness of being single again. This was better than nothing she thought. So she continued her codependent behavior, always trying to keep James happy and comfortable even if it meant sacrificing her own happiness in the process. Eventually, Nancy sought counseling and within a year she felt strong enough to leave James. He had other ideas. The first time Nancy brought up the subject of divorce he laughed at her. Then he threatened her verbally. The day she presented him with divorce papers, he beat her so badly she had to go to the hospital. It seems that despite his lack of love and respect for Nancy, James was addicted to her and the relationship they shared. He also felt that if he couldn't have her, nobody else could.

Eventually, Nancy got away from James even though he stalked her for months—threatening to kill her if she didn't come back. Thankfully, he eventually let go. However, you only have to read the newspapers to realize that such a lethal combination of codependency and narcissism can lead to homicide.

If all this seems complicated, it is. And, to be honest, the only reason it is important is because it makes a difference when it comes to treatment. Recovery for love addiction must include treatment for the underlying personality disorder.

Codependent love addicts, for instance, need a boost in self-esteem and self-acceptance. They must learn to think better of themselves. Narcissistic love addicts, on the other hand, use grandiosity to bolster their low self-esteem and need to come down to earth. They need to learn some humility and how to become "unselfish." Ambivalent Love Addicts need to find a healthy relationship and stay engaged it even when their fear threatens to overwhelm them. Most of all, understanding as much as you can about love addiction will form the basis of your fourth step.

40 Questions
To Help You Determine
If You Are a Love Addict

I f you can answer yes to more than a few of the following questions, you are probably a love addict. Remember that love addiction comes in many forms, so even if you don't answer yes to all of the questions you may still be a love addict.

1.   You are very needy when it comes to relationships.

2.   You fall in love very easily and too quickly.

3.   When you fall in love, you can't stop fantasizing—even to do important things. You can't help yourself.

4.   Sometimes, when you are lonely and looking for companionship, you lower your standards and settle for less than you want or deserve.

5.   When you are in a relationship, you tend to smother your partner.

6.   More than once, you have gotten involved with someone who is unable to commit—hoping he or she will change.

7.   Once you have bonded with someone, you can't let go.

8.   When you are attracted to someone, you will ignore all the warning signs that this person is not good for you.

9.   Initial attraction is more important to you than anything else when it comes to falling in love and choosing a partner. Falling in love over time does not appeal to you and is not an option.

10.   When you are in love, you trust people who are not trustworthy. The rest of the time you have a hard time trusting people.

11.   When a relationship ends, you feel your life is over and more than once you have thought about suicide because of a failed relationship.

12.   You take on more than your share of responsibility for the survival of a relationship.

13. Love and relationships are the only things that interest you.

14. In some of your relationships, you were the only one in love.

15. You are overwhelmed with loneliness when you are not in love or in a relationship.

16. You cannot stand being alone. You do not enjoy your own company.

17 More than once, you have gotten involved with the wrong person to avoid being lonely.

18. You are terrified of never finding someone to love.

19. You feel inadequate if you are not in a relationship.

20. You cannot say no when you are in love or if your partner threatens to leave you.

21. You try very hard to be who your partner wants you to be. You will do anything to please him or her—even abandon yourself (sacrifice what you want, need and value).

22. When you are in love, you only see what you want to see. You distort reality to quell

anxiety and feed your fantasies.

23. You have a high tolerance for suffering in relationships. You are willing to suffer neglect, depression, loneliness, dishonesty—even abuse—to avoid the pain of separation anxiety.

24. More than once, you have carried a torch for someone and it was agonizing.

25. You love romance. You have had more than one romantic interest at a time even when it involved dishonesty.

26. You have stayed with an abusive person.

27. Fantasies about someone you love, even if he or she is unavailable, are more important to you than meeting someone who is available.

28. You are terrified of being abandoned. Even the slightest rejection feels like abandonment and it makes you feel horrible.

29. You chase after people who have rejected you and try desperately to change their minds.

30. When you are in love, you are overly possessive and jealous.

31. More than once, you have neglected family or friends because of your relationship.

32. You have no impulse control when you are in love.

33. You feel an overwhelming need to check up on someone you are in love with.

34. More than once, you have spied on someone you are in love with.

35. You pursue someone you are in love with even if he or she is with another person.

36. If you are part of a love triangle (three people), you believe all is fair in love and war. You do not walk away.

37. Love is the most important thing in the world to you.

38. Even if you are not in a relationship, you still fantasize about love all the time—either someone you once loved or the perfect person who is going to come into your life someday.

39. As far back as you can remember, you have been preoccupied with love and romantic fantasies.

40. You feel powerless when you fall in

love—as if you are in some kind of
trance or under a spell. You lose your
ability to make wise choices.

No Contact Rules

Here are the official Love Addicts Anonymous No
Contact Rules. Everything is a suggestion but it is
like the suggestion to put on your parachute before
you jump. Limited contact is only an option if you
share children or have to process legal papers for a
divorce or business partnership.

When a relationship is over or needs to end because
it is toxic, most healthy people feel loss or sadness,
but eventually they are able to move on. For Love
Addicts, however, the act of "moving on" can be a
seemingly impossible task, steeped in fear and
desperation to hang on. When this is the case, one
must learn to engage in "No Contact" or NC.

The definition of NC is a "Cessation of all contact
between partners . . . and a permanent ending of all
contact between affair partners and the people
surrounding them." But for our purposes, NC is the
act of removing yourself mentally and physically
from your qualifier for the purpose of self-healing.
NC is not a tool to try and win back a PoA or
reconcile. If you find yourself avoiding your PoA or
not answering his calls so as to make him upset or
"want you more," you are missing the point of NC.

NC is a gift you give yourself in order to control your obsessive behavior, overcome your addiction to a person and begin to heal. No contact also means no new hurt. Still, many of us struggle with what NC means, exactly. Below is a list that will help you understand and follow NC:

1. **No Talking in person**: The relationship is over, or you'd like it to be over. This means that you do not engage in talking to your PoA. So often we feel obligated to "say one last thing" or convince someone, through the act of verbal communication, that they should not leave. But a break up is a break up because at least one person does not want to be in the relationship. This needs to be respected. Professing your love, your hatred, or anything else does nothing productive. It will make you look bad, plain and simple. Not only that, but silence is communication. It is saying, "I no longer wish to speak to you." This is VERY hard for a love addict to say. But remember, NC is a gift you give to yourself so that you can heal and become healthy. Remember to focus on your goals. Write them down. You want to learn a healthier way to live and to be. Not talking to your PoA is part of that process of recovery.

2. **No Sex**: Sometimes we use sex as a manipulation to win back Qualifier or to simply feel close via physical contact. But

when the relationship is over, so too are the fringe benefits. Sex after a break up is just sex. NC means no sex with your Qualifier, stranger or friend of the Qualifier (for the purpose of inciting jealousy). Sex without love strips you of self-esteem and dignity. You are worth more.

3. **No Phone calls**: So often we have "one more thing" we need to say. Or we want closure. Or we just want to make that connection or hear their voice. The object of NC is to separate yourself from your Qualifier so that you can heal. So that you can stop the obsessing and recover from a bad relationship. Don't call or leave messages after hours, or call their relatives, their work, etc. It will do absolutely nothing positive. When the relationship is over, so is communication.

4. **No Texts**: One of the hardest things to avoid in today's world is the text message. It has become a relationship backbone. But when the relationship is over, so is communication. Don't text your Qualifier, and don't respond to texts. Delete them as soon as they come in—as hard as that may be—because once you read them, you're hooked and often feel compelled to respond. Sending texts is counterproductive to recovery and healing.

5.   **No E-mails**: Dear Qualifier letters that profess your love, your hatred, or anything else do nothing productive. This type of behavior does very little to initiate closeness with someone who does not want to be in a relationship with you, nor does it help you to break the bonds of a toxic relationship.

6.   **No Letters or Packages**: Don't send back old memories, letters or notes to their door. It crosses boundaries and pushes them away even further. And when you get no response from this, it devastates you. Pack the stuff up and forget about it, or put it in the trash.

7.   **No Instant Messaging**: Instant Messaging, especially when you are both online and your Qualifier is not initiating a conversation, can drive you crazy. There are issues of tone and accusations that are misconstrued in writing. Professing your love, your hatred, anything else to initiate dialogue does nothing productive. It only makes you look bad, plain and simple.

8.   **No Contact from a Distance (stalking)**: When we are obsessed over a Qualifier, we tend to go to great lengths to see them or be near them, even after a break up. This includes going to their favorites places, planning to bump into them, looking for their car, watching them leave in the morning and

more importantly, driving by their home to see if they are there or who might have parked a car in their driveway overnight. This behavior will do nothing but help you find the painful clues you have been looking for but didn't really want to see. This is stalking. It is highly counterproductive to recovery, not to mention dangerous.

9. **No Cyber Stalking**: Perusing social networking sites such as Facebook, MySpace, and Match.com, even eBay, craigslist or Googling, in an attempt to learn more about your Qualifier and "see" what he or she is up to, is against the rules of NC. This type of behavior is stalker-ish. And it does nothing but harshly remind you that they are no longer yours. Delete their profiles or block them. *No good can come from this.*

10. **Do Not Reply**: One of the hardest acts of NC is not responding to pings, emails, phone calls, texts, etc. We believe that if they contact us, we are worthy! They must love us. How can we not respond to that? Some of us respond because we tell ourselves it's rude not to. We don't want to hurt anyone's feelings. But remember, you have a right to place a boundary around yourself and not let certain people in. You have the right to not pick up the phone or reply to a text. It's called discretion. Responding to pings, emails,

phone calls, texts, or any attempt by your Qualifier to contact you are not NC. It breaks the rules and can lead to no good. Block your Qualifier from contacting YOU in every way you can: by phone, text, email, social media, etc.

11. No Contacting the Ex's friends and family: Sometimes we rationalize NC by thinking, "If I'm not directly contacting him (her), I'm safe." So, we continue to forge bonds with friends we shared while dating. But contact with those closest to the Qualifier, their friends, family members, co-workers, is not NC. Asking what they're up to, if they're dating, etc. is still contact. In order to recover we sometimes need to put shared friends on the back burner for a while too in order to heal.

12. No Excessive fantasizing: "No Contact" can be mental and emotional as well as physical. What's the point in following all of the above rules of NC, only to spend your whole day dreaming of the ex?

The idea of NC is NO CONTACT, but some of us simply cannot let go and so we continue the relationship in our minds. This can go on for years (known as torchbearing). Practice thought-stopping. Keep your mind active and busy. Remember that your heart, mind and body are sacred places and also need to experience NC in order to heal.

Note: For those who are unsure, stalking has the following definition and is considered illegal.

"Stalking can be defined as the willful and repeated following, watching, and/or harassing of another person. Most of the time, the purpose of stalking is to attempt to force a relationship with someone who is unwilling or otherwise unavailable. Unlike other crimes, which usually involve one act, stalking is a series of actions that occur over a period of time. Although stalking is illegal, the actions that contribute to stalking are usually legal, such as gathering information, calling someone on the phone, sending gifts, emailing or instant messaging. Such actions by themselves are not usually abusive, but can become abusive when frequently repeated over time."

Limited Contact

LAA is a program of moderation when it comes to love. Our goal is healthy love and healthy relationships. It is not a program of abstinence except when you are obsessed and in withdrawal.

There are times when no contact is impossible. If you have financial ties, share a business, work together, or have children it is really difficult.

Sometimes no contact just does not work because you have unfinished business.

It is important for all of us in LAA to refrain from judging those who choose limited ccontact. The shock of no contact can be just to much for some. Often people need to wean themselves for the sake of their sanity. Other times, with a child, limited contact, with healthy boundaries, is the norm. Withdrawal is harder for some than others. Codependents, especially, may opt for limited contact because their is a family and/or extended family involved.

Limited contact involves healthy boundaries. Do not fool yourself into believing going back into your codependency or love addiction is just limited contact.

Underlying Issues

Love Addicts need to accept the fact that we have underlying issues. Nothing can change until we acknowledge that we have a problem.

This is the First Step in Love Addicts Anonymous. Like the step suggests, it helps to admit that we are powerless for now and need help. Take the time to announce this at a meeting or to your Sponsor. Most of all be fearlessly honest with yourself and be humble. Remeber that "pride goes before a fall," and after a fall as well. Pride has no place at this crucial time of our life.

Suggestions

Identify the underlying issues. If we do not remember our childhood, we can look at photographs, talk to siblings, friends or our parents who knew us as a child. Meditate or analyze our dreams. The truth will come out if we want it to. Once you are willing to remember, you may start having flashbacks. Here is a list of underlying issues:

- chronic insecurity
- chronic anxiety
- depression
- feelings of alienation
- loneliness
- a profound hunger for love
- an exaggerated fear of abandonment and rejection
- feelings of deprivation
- feelings of emptiness
- confusion or fear when love is available
- anxiety when things are going well
- some kind of addiction

Talk about what we remember. Talk at closed meetings. Talk with our Sponsor. Talk to a therapist. Talk to a friend. Find someone we can trust and who can either sympathize or even empathize with what we have gone through. Don't stop talking until we have emptied out our pain. Do not for a minute think we are talking too much or bothering someone. We are in recovery. This exercise is not a conversation. We do not have to ask how our listener is feeling. We have to talk and let things we have forgotten seep up from our unconscious mind.

Write in our journal about what we are discovering. As we write, marvelous things we have forgotten will spill out onto the page. This can be a personal journal or we can share it with others. We must pour our heart out onto the page and further this process of discovery.

Feel all of our emotions as they come up without drinking or using other unhealthy mood-altering experiences. Addicts don't like to feel painful emotions. We like to self-medicate or distract ourselves. We like to hide our feelings or stuff them or lash out at others to release them. Do not let shame stop us from feeling the emotions. There is no emotion that should be ashamed of. Even if we did something we regret because of our feelings, we can deal with that when we get to the Ninth Step. For now we must just feel. This was the very first thing we hear at a support group: "If we want to recover we have to feel our feelings."

Grieve what we went through. If we can't do this directly, imagine that our inner child was hurt, and do for him/her what we cannot do for ourselves.

Grieving is similar to my suggestion above. We feel the loss of our childhood. We wish we had not suffered so much. We wish we could have had loving parents. We want what we did not have because we were just a little children and deserved more.

Get angry for awhile if we have spent a lifetime suppressing our emotions. This is an important step in the process. It is part of letting go. When we get angry we are being honest. We are not making excuses for our parents. We are feeling what all children need to feel to survive and yet were not allowed to feel. For more about anger, see Susan Anderson's book: *The Journey from Abandonment and Healing.*

Do not get lost in the anger. Anger is a "double edged sword." It is part of the process, not the process itself. As soon as we are able, move on and put this all into perspective. Were the people who hurt us abused or neglected? What about their grandparents? If we are a parent did we pass down the pain to our children to ease our own burdens.

After we put things into perspective, consider forgiving these people. To forgive means to let go of resentment. We do not have to like them, associate with them, or let them continue to hurt us. This suggestion is controversial. Some professionals say it is not necessary or might even be harmful. AA says it is an absolute imperative.

We believe it is important. Nothing changes in our lives until we forgive people.

Accept what happened to us. How do we do this? We can't do it right away. We can't do it when we want to. We can't do it while we are in the angry stage. We will do it when we are ready. We can push ourselves a little, but we must be patient. Tell ourselves: these were the cards we were dealt. Maybe something good will come out of this. According to AA: "Acceptance is the answer to all our problems today. When I am disturbed, it is because I find some person, place, thing or situation—some fact of my life—unacceptable to me, and I can find no serenity until I accept this person, place, thing or situation as being exactly the way it is supposed to be at this moment."

Move on. This is the fun part. We drop all of this. We create a new life. We embrace our present and dream about the future. We live our life of abundance. Of course, the past will come back to haunt us now and then because this is the way the brain works, especially when we go home for the holidays to the scene of the crime. However, as time goes on, the pain of the past will lessen and come up less often to disrupt our new life in recovery.

Take care of ourselves. Do for ourselves what our parents could not or would not do. What this means is a little pampering, forgiving ourselves, and having fun.

Be grateful for this process that is going to free us, change us, and bring us a brighter tomorrow. Gratitude, according to AA imperative. It takes us out of our own misery. If we don't feel grateful, "act as if." Fake it until we make it. Once we discover how "we can be" grateful even when we don't "feel" grateful we will never stop.

Celebrate our victories and hard work. Use our imagination. What did we do when we graduated or got married or even won the lottery? Celebrate our recovery as well. Celebrate God if we are a believer.

Pass all of this on to the next poor soul looking for help–anyway we can. It is fun and good for our self-esteem. This is the 12th step and while touted as a suggestion, it is like suggesting we put on a parachute when we jump out of a plane.

Remember that we cannot do this alone. Our steps use the word "we" for a reason. We can seek help in a 12-Step program. We can go to therapy. We can ask a friend to help us. The only requirement is that this person be an enlightened witness–someone who will have compassion and understanding about our addictions and our struggle to get better.

Recovery

In Love Addicts Anonymous, recovery is a state in which you are able to love yourself as much as you love others. You are guided by a power greater than yourself who knows what is best for you. You are growing and changing. Love is a want not a need. Romantic love enhances your life but does not determine your self-worth. Most of the time you are serene and think clearly when it comes to relationships. Your behavior is sane and marked by emotional sobriety. You do not "love" too much. You do not "do" too much for others. You do not chase after unavailable people. You do not put up with ambivalent people like narcissists or seductive withholders. You have researched healthy relation-ships so you know what your goals are. You stay close to people who are also in recovery in order to avoid relapse. You never take recovery for granted or become complacent. Love addiction is "cunning, baffling, and powerful." It lies in wait for us when we let our guard down. Above all else, you put your well being ahead of your romantic attachments. You understand that romantic love is not enough to sustain you. It is like a flower without roots. You need love and compatibility with someone who can reciprocate.

You should be able to agree with most of these statements.

1. I know I am lovable despite my shortcomings.

2. I have self-discipline.

3. I am honest.

4. I am true to my values.

5. I am responsible.

6. I know myself—what my values are and what I want.

7. I can talk about my feelings.

8. I do not feel needy.

9. I am not afraid of being single.

10. When I am alone I do not feel lonely.

11. I have an active, full life.

12. When I am in an intimate relationship I still have other interests.

13. I do nice things for myself as well as others.

14. I can receive as well as give.

15. I do creative things.

16. I do not compare myself to others.

17. I can stand up for myself.

18. I can say "no" when it is appropriate.

19. I am growing and making progress in my life.

20. I am contributing to the world.

21. I have surrounded myself with healthy people.

22. I feel connected to myself and the world.

23. I feel loved by many people.

24. I feel like a whole person.

25. I do not like rejection, but I can handle it.

26. I do not over-react to criticism by attacking or getting defensive.

27. I have processed most of my feelings about my dysfunctional childhood.

28. I am not angry all of the time about my past.

29. I do not feel guilty all of the time about the mistakes I have made.

30. I can handle adversity without falling apart.

31. I can end an unhealthy relationship.

32. I can stick with a healthy relationship.

33. I do not feel suicidal when relationships end.

34. I have some stress-management techniques.

35. I feel good about myself.

36. I have balance in my life. I know how to find the middle ground.

37. I know what I want, but I am not addicted to getting it.

38. I have structure, but I am also flexible.

39. I have trustworthy people in my life.

40. I do not have to control everything and everybody in my life.

41. I have worked through my sexual hangups. I know what healthy sex is.

42. I can argue with someone without attacking them or give them the silent treatment.

Working the 12-Steps

Step 1: We admitted we were powerless over love, romance, fantasies and relationships—that our lives had become unmanageable.

"We" reminds us that we are not alone. "Admitted" refers to honesty between ourselves and others. "Powerless" refers to helplessness at this moment in time. It is not meant to mean that were are always powerless. "Our lives had become unmanageable" means that we have lost control.

This step is about honesty and humility. We swallow our pride and get honest about where our love addiction has taken us. Humility is the first step in many journeys of transformation. It is a rite of passage. Please note that we are only powerless at this stage in our recovery because we have isolated from God and our fellow human beings. The power to recover comes back to us as we reach out for help and continue to work the rest of the steps.

Step 2: Came to believe that a power greater than ourselves could restore us to sanity.

LAA is a spiritual program. We believe that we cannot restore ourselves but must be restored by divine intervention. In other words, we cannot recover by ourselves, we need help. This help comes in the form of some higher power, whether that be a deity or the energy of the group. This step is about hope. It follows the very painful admission that we [by ourselves] are powerless. So be hopeful. Whether you pray to God or reach out to others, don't try to get better in isolation. Reach out and have faith that your distorted thinking and behavior will be transformed into a healthy way of thinking and behaving.

Step 3: [We] Made a decision to turn our will and our lives over to the care of God as we understood God.

If we are "powerless" over love and our lives are unmanageable, and God, as we understand God, can restore us to sanity then it is best we turn our life and our will over to God so that he can mend our broken hearts.

Note that God can mean some benevolent force in the universe or the God within which knows what is best for us. Note that we turn ourselves over to the "care" of God. Note that this is a decision which must be followed by action. Just how do we turn our will over? We commit to change. We look to our recovery friends for an example of a sane way to love and we follow in their footsteps. We find the right path through trial and error. Our only guide is the belief that God wants us to be healthy and happy. If we are not, then we are going in the wrong direction. God will lead you to people and books

which will help you. God will lead you forward.
Without God we are defenseless against our
addiction. You do not have to be religious to
believe in goodness. God is goodness. God is spirit.
The spiritual approach to recovery may be hard on
some people. But it is tried and true. Herbert
Spencer said "Ignorance is contempt prior to
investigation." Try this approach if you have failed
to get better on your own or with therapy alone.
There are legions of people for whom this approach
has worked. Surrender (to be free from addiction) to
an old familiar God or to a new God of your choice.
Don't be afraid. You will meet others on this path.
You will not be alone.

*Step 4: Made a searching and fearless moral
inventory of ourselves.*

The more we know about the problem the more we
know what to change. We cannot be too general.
We cannot just decide to change our lives. We must
break this down into manageable pieces. We must
change our values about love and how we think and
behave. For example, love is not worth dying for
(value), we will survive the end of a relationship
(thinking), and we will not chase after unavailable
people (behavior). An inventory can include your
history of relationships but it should also focus on
exactly what you want to change about yourself,
like low self-esteem and shame-based thinking,
feeling, and acting. Take a list of symptoms from
any good book about love addiction and write about

the ones that apply to you. Don't forget to list the things about yourself that you want to keep and expand on. Inventories should include the good and the bad. Discuss in your inventory the people you have hurt. Later, in the eighth step, you will be creating a list of such people. What drove you to hurt these people? What things are you later going to ask God to remove? It is traditional to write out your fourth step, but this is not mandatory. Some people do a fourth and fifth step in therapy on a weekly basis How you do this step is unimportant. The only important thing is that you do it.

Step 5: Admitted to God, to ourselves, and another to human being the exact nature of our wrongs.

Once you complete your fourth step inventory it is time to give it away. LAA is a spiritual program, so naturally we invite God. Our relationship with God comes first. We can take time in prayer and meditation to open up and communicate with the God of our understanding about the exact nature of our wrongs. Then we invite and connect with another human being who will actively listen to our inventory without judging, a person who feels safe to us. This person will be someone we respect, someone you can trust sharing this information with and someone who will be empathetic. Set aside as much time as you need to complete the process. Step five instructs us to admit the exact nature of our wrongs to ourselves at heart level and then connect with another human being to share what we have written. Looking at the harm we have caused ourselves and others, may put us in touch with the exact nature of our wrongs as never before. As we do this, we can see the pain caused by our denial. An honest Fifth Step supports us in our recovery and helps us understand why our lives were unmanageable. Admitting our wrongs to ourselves helps break through to greater honesty, self-awareness and acceptance. Open your heart, your mind, and your soul to this process. Admit everything. Be courageous. Don't take anything to the grave. After the fifth step, take some time to be alone and to be introspective. Step Five opens the door to truth and freedom. Step Five teaches us to be vulnerable and to trust. Step Five is about letting go.

Step 6: Were entirely ready to have God remove these defects of character.

The key words in this step are "ready" and "God." Sometimes were are not ready, even though we want to be, and other times we want to do it ourselves without God. Love addiction is insidious. It does not let go of us and we cannot let go of it without help. Our character defects (bad habits) are also difficult to let go of. We may like some of them and hold on despite the fact that they are undermining our self-esteem. For example lying and stealing may be lucrative habits that we aren't ready to let go of. If we have thoroughly worked the steps up to now, there should be some willingness to become a better person. This is enough. We do not have to work this step perfectly despite the word "entirely." This step is a bridge to the next and so if you are willing at all you can proceed.

While fear and habit hold us back, we may also still be of the belief that we can become better people by sheer will power. If you still believe this then you must go back and work the previous steps again. Members of LAA are people who believe we need the power of God to lift our obsessions. Not everyone needs divine intervention, but we do. We are "powerless" without help and without our Higher Power. So admit to yourself and another human being that you are ready to have God remove your shortcomings and move on to Step 7. If you can't do this then stay with this step until you are ready. The day will come when you see that your character defects are standing between you and your happiness and you will be happy to ask God to help you surrender them.

Step 7: Humbly asked him [God] to remove our shortcomings.

In the Twelve Steps and Twelve Traditions, written by the co-founder of Alcoholics Anonymous, it says, "The whole emphasis of Step Seven is on humility." This is because it is through a recognition that we need help that we are healed. We simply cannot do this alone. We cannot change ourselves through will power alone. Willingness has its place, but it must be in conjunction with divine grace. For those who have tried again and again to get well on their own this step will be the answer to their prayers. There is hope.

There is a catch to this prayer. Your shortcomings will not just disappear like magic. More likely you will just be given opportunities to learn.

The other thing about this step is that God will only remove the shortcomings that he feels stand in the way of your development. Many of the things that you don't like about yourself will remain untouched. This keeps us humble. One thing for sure, however, is that recovery is God's will for us. Any shortcoming that gets in the way of that will be removed. So ask God for help and then work with him. Be patient. Have faith!

Step 8: Made a list of all persons we had harmed, and became willing to make amends to them all.

It is easy to see love addicts as victims because we get hurt so much by our disease, but often our addiction takes over and we put ourselves ahead of others. We might neglect our friends and family. We may put a lover ahead of our children. Perhaps under the stress of our addiction we lashed out or abused someone. Maybe we stole money to take care of someone we were addicted to. The degree to which we hurt others was explored in our fourth step inventory. Now we must take that inventory and make a list of the people we have harmed and become willing to make amends to them. There will be people on this list who also hurt us, but that is irrelevant. We must only be concerned about our own actions and making amends for them. Many people get stuck on this step because they are holding on to old resentments, but recovery demands that we heal by reaching out to those we have hurt because of our love addiction. Don't get ahead of yourself and worry about step 9. Just make your list and ask God for the willingness to continue cleaning house.

Step 9. Made direct amends to such people wherever possible, except when to do so would injure them or others.

Once you have finished your list of people you have harmed, and are willing to make amends to them (step 8), it is time to do so—unless going to them would reveal information that would devastate them. This step takes time and you can continue to work the rest of the steps while keeping this step on your calendar as a long-term project.

You can make amends in writing or in person. But remember that no one is obligated to accept your apology. If you owe people money, and cannot afford to pay them, then set up a payment plan. Just be sincere and most people will respond in a positive way.

If the person you want to make amends to is unavailable, or dead, make a *living* amends. This means doing for someone else what you would have done with this person if you had it to do over again. Give money to charity if you cannot repay someone money you owe. If you neglected your children, because of your love addiction, then make a fresh start with your grandchildren. If you hurt friends who are no longer in your life, find new friends and be good to them.

Step 9 is hard work. It takes time. But it feels good and clears away the wreckage of the past. After you have completed this step, it is time to forgive yourself and let go of the past.

Step 10. Continue to take personal inventory and when we were wrong promptly admitted it.

Step 10 is a continuation of the 4th and 9th steps. Not only must we be introspective about our current shortcomings, and share them with God and another human being, if we have acted out in some way, we must go to the person we have harmed and quickly apologize.

Some people do this step every day after they have retired. They look over the day that has just passed and do a quick inventory. Others only work this step when something noticeable has happened. Some people do this in writing. Others don't. It is up to you do integrate this step into the discipline of your recovery program. How you do this step is less important than doing it.

This step is meant for events that occur in your current life. If you want to do more work about past events and fear-based emotions such as resentments, you can go back and do another 4th step inventory.

Step 10 is one of the maintenance steps. It helps us keep the serenity we have already gotten from the others steps. It helps keep our recovery strong. Maintaining recovery is as important at finding it. Regression is always waiting for us without proper vigilance.

Step 11: Sought through prayer and meditation to improve our conscious contact with God as we understood God, praying only for knowledge of God's will for us and the power to carry that out.

All relationships get better when you pay attention to them. The eleventh steps encourages you to improve your relationship with God using prayer (talking to God) and meditation (listening to God), but you can also use other spiritual disciplines such as study, solitude, humility, submission, service, confession, worship, celebration etc. (anything that brings you closer to God).

Not only is it a good thing to get closer to God, you should learn to end each prayer with "thy will be done." The reason you only want to know God's will for you is simply that God knows what is best for you. You only have an idea of what might make you happy. God knows you better than you know yourself and you want what he/she wants for you.

Since we are so attached to our own ideas of what will make us happy, we must also ask for the strength to carry out God's will for us. The journey may have a rocky start. God may want us to do things we don't want to do or are afraid to do.

Praying is an art form and LAA believes that this eleventh step way of praying will get the best results.

Step 12: Having had a spiritual awakening as the result of these Steps, we tried to carry this message to others, and to practice these principles in all our affairs.

One of the indications that you have had a genuine spiritual awakening is that you want to share this experience with others. You want them to be as happy as you are. You want to help them have a similar experience. This step suggests that we do just that, that we "carry the message." It is also a well known spiritual principle that to keep our own spirituality strong and fresh we must "pass it on." So what we call 12th step work is for you as well as for others.

How you carry the message is up to you. Any kind of service helps. You may donate your time and money to LAA. You may sponsor someone. Every time you answer a post on the message board you are practicing the 12th step.

Recovery is about change. Sometimes the changes are obvious when you are in a support group. But the support group is like a hot house protecting delicate flowers. The real test is when you go out into the world. Can you practice what you have learned in LAA when you go to work or socialize with your friends? Can your recovery stand up against your next romantic relationship? This is the question.

Self-Esteem

To find happiness and avoid relapse, love addicts and codependents must build their self-esteem because low-self esteem robs love addicts the confidence they need to remain single until the right man comes along.

Love addicts with low-esteem are needy and quickly become infatuated. They settle for less than they deserve, and they avoid cutting their losses because without self-esteem they are so lonely. Not to mention haunted by their past.

Low-self esteem feeds love addiction, it might be

more helpful to elaborate on what high self esteem does for recovering love addicts. It helps them because now they can:

- Stand alone until love is a "want," not a "need."

- Discover a willingness to grow and change (maturation, self- actualization).

- Make their own needs a priority.

- Look after themselves enough to make life enjoyable.

- Find joy in life.

- Get through the hard times.

- Discover their authentic (true) self.

- Wait for the right person to come along.

- Overcome loneliness.

- Heal the wounds of childhood.

- Develop self-control.

- Love others in a healthy way.

- Experience the joy of solitude.

- Displace depression.

- Reduce anxiety.

- Protect themselves from abusive and manipulative people, i.e. narcissists.

- Want to be creative (what Joseph Campbell calls "follow your bliss").

Low self-esteem is the by-product of a difficult childhood. If a child is neglected, abused, or abandoned, they blame themselves even if they are dealing with a problem that is obviously that of the parent. Even something like depression is internalized by the child who takes responsibility for it. We call this (from the child's perspective) "mom sad; me bad."

Later, children may mature to the point that they can put the blame on the inadequate parent, but by then the damage may already be done. The child is self-alienated, ashamed, or just lacking in the confidence we need to thrive and avoid dependency on other people.

It isn't always easy to measure the relationship between the degree of neglect or abuse, and one's level of self-esteem. Usually, the more you were neglected or abused the less self-esteem you have. However, this is not the only factor that should be considered when trying to measure the impact of neglect and abuse on self-esteem. One should also consider the level of sensitivity each child is born with and any insulation they might have had while growing up.

Because of the causal relationship between self-alienation, shame, low self-esteem and love addiction, LAA would like to suggest a cognitive behavioral approach to feel better about ourselves.

Steps to Building Up Self-esteem

1. Adopt an *attitude* of self-acceptance or self-love. This means really understanding that you are a worthy person despite your shortcomings. This is a mindset. Then, once you have a general acceptance of your worth as a human being, spend some time focusing on your specific attributes. This enhances your self-worth. Just don't get carried away.

2. Affirmations are an important part of building ourselves up to a level of optimum confidence. I like affirmations like "I'm ok; I am a work in progress; be patient God is not through with me yet. Affirmations that put myself in true perspective—not better than others but certainly as good as.

3. You can't burn down a house and feel good about yourself. You must earn some of yourself. Consider self-respect from self-discipline, being responsible, honoring your own value system, and handling adversity well.

4. Self-respect, which is a kind of conditional love, does not necessarily contradict the notion that you should love yourself unconditionally. Both concepts are important to maintain self-esteem. You must try to find the balance between loving yourself unconditionally and pushing yourself to do things that will engender self-respect.

5. Pick your friends carefully. You have no choice about your co-workers and family, but friends are a choice, one you did not have as a child.

6. Get to know yourself and then place a high value on who you are.

7. Stop trying to be perfect. No one is perfect.

8. We value what we take care of. So take care of yourself. Discard negative people and unhealthy relationships. (This includes pampering.)

9. Do nice things for other people but don't over do it. Altruism builds self-esteem but too much giving is co-dependent.

10. Stop comparing yourself to others. You are special in your own way and this is the attitude you must have about yourself.

11. If you have a monopoly on giving to build a false sense of self-esteem, learn how to receive. For instance, stop dismissing compliments and returning gifts. Let the love come in.

12. Everyone has a gift. Find it and spend time doing it. Then find an audience.

13. Many love addicts have a hard time standing up for themelves. This has to change. So start setting limits (saying no), expressing your opinion, walking away from neglect or abuse, being assertive when appropriate, and no longer apologizing when you haven't done anything wrong.

14. Prepare yourself mentally for those times when people try to drag you down (people you can't avoid like co-workers). Learn how to keep from taking them so seriously, as well as how to filter out inappropriate criticism.

15. Spiritual-minded people can try seeing themselves as a special child to an omnipotent diety. I know for sure I am a child of God, and as they say in Alcoholics Anonym;ous, "God does not make any junk."

Low self-esteem goes hand and hand with love addiction. Therefore it is obvious, in recovery, how important it is to build yourself up and surround yourself with people who validate you. The most common mistake love addicts make, as well as moving too quickly, is to let their current partner pick up where their abusive and neglectful parents left off. Be diligent. Be thoughtful. Keep working on it. The most genuine and long-lasting form of happiness comes from loving yourself and demanding respect from other or walking away if you don't get it.

Dating in Recovery

Many people search for love and end up with the wrong person. This is because they fall in love and bond before they know what they are getting. LAA has prepared a list of characteristics that a person should have in their relationship before they become serious. Carry it around for you and check what you have against what you need to have a successful relationship.

The most important thing is availability. Your partner should be willing to move if you are long distance and they must also be available emotionally and spiritually. No avoidants or ambivalent people. One of our members found a woman with everything on his list and after he was in love and ready to move forward he discovered that she was not willing to relocate and neither was he. They lived in different countries.

So many of the important things on this list should come up fairly early. If you want to date then go slowly. If you want to end up married with children then you must find out if this is an option before you fall in love. Availability is EVERYTHING.

LAA Dating Plan

What to Look for in a Healthy Relationship . . .

1. Honesty that engenders trust.

2. Readiness for a relationship (both partners).

3. The willingness to negotiate or compromise.

4. Self-awareness—this means both partners knowing who they are and what they want.

5. Self-esteem—this means both partners feeling good about themselves.

6. Communication skills.

This means:

-   Asking for what you want, but not being addicted to getting it.

- Fighting fair. (This means expressing your opinion without attacking the other person.)

- Reporting your feelings.

- Saying what you mean (not beating around the bush).

- Listening, as well as talking.

7. Sexual compatibility. This means similar values and preferences.

8. There should be a recognition of the fact that there are 4 people in the relationship—2 adults and 2 children (1 inner child per adult).

This means:

- That childhood wounds will probably be triggered and sensitivity strategies must be created.

- That rituals from your family of origin must be re-negotiated and new rituals created as a couple.

- And, finally, that the wounded inner child must be kept in check. (In other words, love your inner child, but don't give him or her the keys to the car.)

9. Similar (but not necessarily identical) values about such issues as money, religion, monogamy, and parenting. This avoids needless conflict. Still, you don't have to agree about everything—just what's important to you.

10. Patience and tolerance, but you should never tolerate abuse.

11. It is important to accept the fact that there will be days when the relationship seems very ordinary or even boring. Many people tend to have an "all or nothing" mentality. They either want a relationship to be exciting all the time, or they live with unbearable pain rather than move on. Healthy relationships are sometimes lukewarm.

12. The willingness to substitute "influencing" for "controlling."

This means:

-   Saying something once and then letting it go.

-   It also means being a role-model instead of nagging someone to change.

13. The willingness to keep your personality boundaries (even when you feel like losing yourself in the other person). This is how we maintain our self-esteem.

14. Devotion. How can an intimate relationship feel good if we aren't special to each other.

15. Quality time together. At the same time, you want to set aside time for personal interests. Look for balance.

16. Knowing when to stay and when to leave. This means staying when things are going well (and you feel like running), and being willing to let go of the relationship if it is unhealthy.

17. It is also important to have compatibility and "ease" in a relationship. At the same time it must be understood that no relationship is perfect. (Compatibility comes from being alike or from having a high tolerance for your partner's differences.)

18. The willingness to face your problems (without over-reacting).

19. Respect and admiration, but there should also be an understanding that your partner will not always look good to you.

20. Reciprocity (give and take), but you should also be willing to make sacrifices now and then.

21. Realistic expectations about how much of your happiness should come from the relationship—not too much and not too little.

Progression of Relationship

Before you get started develop a fulfilling relationship with yourself before you attempt to have a romantic relationship. Romantic feelings can be like a tidal wave sweeping you out to sea if you are not securely tied to a relationship with yourself. Many of you may want to be swept out to sea, but this is not really healthy; and sometimes it is even dangerous.

Selection:

- Take your time;

- Do everything you can to keep from being blinded by your emotions;

- Know what you don't want (people who trigger your dysfunctional behavior);

- Look for someone healthy, and observe them objectively before you plunge in;

- Look for someone who does not have to change very much too please you; but don't be too picky. Find the middle ground.

- Know what you do want. Make a list of the things that are mandatory and the things that are optional. Prioritize your list.

Dating:

- This is when you find out what this person is really like—any false fronts should crumble.

- Be yourself—you want someone to know who you really are;

- Measure your compatibility during this time;

- Establish trust;

- Hold off on sex if it blinds you to what this person is really like, and keep a lid on any budding romantic feelings (you may feel them, but don't give them a lot of power by fantasizing too much);

- Be willing to change your mind if you usually "cling" to unhealthy people and be willing to hang in there if you usually "run."

Friendship:

- See if you can relax and have fun together;

- See if you can count on this person;

- Continue to see if there is enough compatibility to sustain the relationship;

- Build a strong foundation for a future romantic relationship.

· Courtship:

- This is friendship combined with romance.

- Romantic feelings can now have a free reign—see if they mix well with the friendship;

- You can let romantic love blossom now—you don't have to put a lid on your feelings anymore;

- Now you can test your readiness for intimacy; this is usually the time when a fear of intimacy comes up—if you have any.

Commitment:

- Now things are getting serious;

- Set ground rules for the relationship;

- Discuss things like:

    * Fidelity
    * Growing closer
    * The future

* How much time you will have for each other

...anything that is important to you.

Partnership: (This used to be called marriage, but now the wedding ceremony is optional.)

During a partnership you should:

- Maintain what you have established up to now;

- Honor the values you have in common;

- Grow as a couple, as well as individuals;

- Get to really know each other and experience intimacy. (Intimacy comes from revealing yourself to a non-judgmental partner.)

Switch:

At any point in the progression of a relationship, one partner may experience a fear of intimacy and pull back. Don't panic. Give your partner some space. However, if he or she does not come around in a few weeks, you should move on. (This is discussed more fully in *A Fine Romance* by Judith Sills.)

LAA wants to give you a word of encouragement and a warning. Intimate relationships are wonderful and something to aspire to. They can enhance your life in unbelievable ways. They can be very fulfilling and help you grow to your full potential. But always remember that they are a "want" not a "need." Your self-esteem should never depend on finding someone special.

Also, love (as attraction and desire) is not enough. Love that follows a careful selection, and is coupled with a willingness to work hard and extend yourself is also necessary.

Finally, you must not become slaves to the myth that preferential love will always span an entire lifetime. Only spiritual love lasts forever. Therefore, as you change, your relationship will change; and sometimes (but not always) it will fade away. You should not be discouraged by this. Change is part of life. It is what makes life interesting.

Cross Talk

It is suggested that we do not crosstalk in LAA meetings. Crosstalk can be defined as giving advice, asking questions, referring to another person by name, directing comments to a specific individual, or commenting on what another person has shared. All of these things make it difficult for some of us to express our true feelings. Furthermore, please maintain the quiet of the room by not making inappropriate or overt responses to what others are saying. Non-verbal acknowledgments, such as nodding your head, is acceptable. Even laughter can be misinterpreted so be cautious. Finally, do not whisper in side conversations. Thank you!

Note: There is crosstalk on the LAA Message Board and you may ask permission after the meeting to offer a member some positive feedback.

12 Steps of LAA

1. We admitted we were powerless over love, romance, fantasies and relationships—that our lives had become unmanageable.

2. Came to believe that a Power greater than ourselves could restore us to sanity.

3. Made a decision to turn our will and our lives over to the care of God as we understood God.

4. Made a searching and fearless moral inventory of ourselves.

5. Admitted to God, to ourselves, and to another human being the exact nature of our wrongs.

6. Were entirely ready to have God remove all these defects of character.

7. Humbly asked God to remove our shortcomings.

8. Made a list of all persons we had harmed, and became willing to make amends to them all.

9. Made direct amends to such people wherever possible, except when to do so would injure them or others.

10. Continued to take personal inventory and when we were wrong promptly admitted it.

11. Sought through prayer and meditation to improve our conscious contact with God as we understood God, praying only for knowledge of God's will for us and the power to carry that out.

12. Having had a spiritual awakening as the result of these Steps, we tried to carry this message to others, and to practice these principles in all our affairs.

12 Promises of LAA

1. I have a new sense of freedom because I am letting go of the past.

2. I am hopeful about my future relationships.

3.   I can be attracted to someone without falling in love overnight, and I can fall in love without obsessing.

4.   If love does overwhelm me I do not act out in addictive ways.

5.   I can tell the difference between fantasies and reality.

6.   I do not have to control the ones I love nor let them control me.

7.   I experience relationships one at a time and I do not get involved with "unavailable" people.

8.   If my basic needs are not being met, I can end my relationship.

9.   I can leave anyone who is abusing me either verbally or physically.

10. I do not do for others what they should be doing for themselves.

11. I love myself as much as I love others.

12. I look to my Higher Power for strength, guidance, and the willingness to change.

12 Traditions of LAA

1. Our common welfare should come first; personal recovery depends upon LAA unity.

2. For our group purpose, there is but one ultimate authority—a loving Higher Power as expressed in our group conscience. Our leaders are but trusted servants; they do not govern.

3. The only requirement for membership in LAA is a desire to recover from love addiction.

4. Each group should remain autonomous except in matters affecting other groups or LAA as a whole.

5. Each group has but one primary purpose—to carry the message of recovery to those who still suffer.

6. An LAA group ought never endorse, finance, or lend the LAA name to any related facility or outside enterprise, lest problems of money, property and prestige divert us from our primary purpose.

7. A LAA group ought to be fully self-supporting, declining outside contributions.

8. Love Addicts Anonymous should remain forever non-professional, but our service centers may employ special workers.

9. LAA, as such, ought never be organized; but we may create service boards or committees directly responsible to those they serve.

10. LAA has no opinion on outside issues; hence the LAA name ought never be drawn into public controversy.

11. Our public relations policy is based on attraction rather than promotion; we need always maintain personal anonymity at the public level.

12. Anonymity is the spiritual foundation of all our traditions, ever reminding us to place principles before personalities.

12 Steps to a Stronger Spiritual Life

1. Meditation: Get quiet and listen to God through your feelings and intuition.

2. Prayer: Talk to God (out loud or in your head) as if you were talking to a close, personal friend.

3. Humility: God is a Higher Power. You are a lesser power. You know this. You are humbled by it.

4. Study: Read, write, learn, listen.

5. Simplicity: Slow down. Experience and appreciate the simple things in life—nature, music, friends.

6. Solitude: Take some time to be alone and listen to your own inner music.

7. Submission: Surrender everything to God—as you understand God.

8. Love: Learn to love yourself as well as God and others

9. Service: Reach out to people in need and give of yourself and your resources.

10. Confession: Find someone you can trust and confide your deepest, darkest secrets to them. Release the shame.

11. Worship: Be in awe of your Higher Power. Bow your head—metaphorically or literally. Be thankful for the grace that has been freely given to you.

12. Celebration: Be grateful! Raise your hands in joy and celebration. Sing, dance and be merry.

Spirituality

We want to conclude this book with some thoughts about spirituality and recovery.

Many of us are not born spiritually conscious; we wake up to a spiritual way of life only after a crisis. We make a conscious decision to follow a spiritual path, and then we become spiritual people. So what is spirituality to Love Addicts Anonymous?

Well, in the simplest of terms, it is a shift in consciousness which brings about a willingness to CHANGE. We begin doing things differently. We think differently, communicate differently, love differently. In doing so, we become spiritual beings.

Changing is a slow process. As they like to say in 12-Step programs, it is "spiritual progress, rather than spiritual perfection."

Our best friend on the journey of change is our spiritual intuition because she whispers in our ear at just the right moment. She tells us through feelings and insight what to say, what to do, or how to feel; even if we don't want to say, do or feel the way she wants us to.

In listening to this inner voice, we find the courage and strength to change. We could list all of the changes you might make, but figuring them all out is part of your journey. We learn what we have to change in our fourth step inventory. Also, if you read and listen to the right people you will learn what has to be changed. Here is are the steps you must take and the obstacles you must overcome.

- All change begins with willingness which is the gift of spirituality.

- Stay focused on yourself. You are the one that needs to change, not other people.

- Watch out for denial, defense mechanisms, perfectionism, rigidity, fear, bonding to old habits, love of familiarity, stubbornness, and depression. All of these things inhibit change.

- Be ready to suffer. Some changes are painful.

- If you change your mind, you change your life. So always strive to turn negative thinking into positive thoughts. This is an effort for many of us, but not impossible. Embrace the clichés. There is a silver lining to every cloud. There is a "bright side" to everything. We just have to look for it.

- Gratitude is not a feeling. It is a way of looking at things that leads to a feeling of appreciation. We cannot change unless we are grateful. It is the antidote to resentment and self-pity. When something goes wrong, make a gratitude list. Write down and ruminate on all the things you are grateful for—no matter how small.

- Make a list of the most important changes that you have to make. You can stick the list on the refrigerator or hide it in the drawer. God does not care. Just remember to look at it once in awhile and check off a change or two before you get much older.

- Face your shortcomings. Be honest with yourself about your weaknesses. Then get honest with another person. Tell someone what needs to be changed about yourself. Confession is good for the soul, but it is also the beginning of change.

- Some people have been wounded by the past. They will not be able to change without the guidance of a counselor. Don't be afraid of this. God created the science of psychology just as he created the great surgeons who heal our bodies.

- Open yourself up to loving yourself. You are like a beautiful plant that is withered if you

lack self-esteem. Let spirituality shine upon
you and then grow toward that light.

Progress

No matter how much we move forward, there is
always more work to do. Therefore, in this life we
must settle for progress or what I call living in the
shadow of perfection. Let this be enough. Make
peace with it if you are a perfectionist. After all, as
long as we are imperfect we need God on our side,
and he/she is wonderful company.

Members'
Stories

Introduction

Change is important and the process of change begins with honesty. The honesty is the willingness to admit aloud that you have a problem or weakness; that you have done things you regret. The honesty takes on an even deeper meaning when you tell your story. This is never easy, but as you listen to yourself describe your experience with weakness, you will gain a new awareness of how you have gotten off track. This, in turn, will help you understand what needs to be changed as your transformation unfolds.

Telling your story not only helps you, it helps others. As people listen to you, they often hear their own story and find out they are not alone. This provides an overwhelming sense of well-being. It dissipates the shame and jump-starts the transformation process.

Since the publication of the book *Alcoholics Anonymous* in 1939, stories have been important to those in 12-Step programs. Love Addicts Anonymous is now publishing the stories of those who have found recovery for love addiction.

\

The Hungry Heart

Today I am a SURVIVOR. Before my recovery began, however, I was an addict. My drug of choice was romantic love. It kind of crept up on me. In the beginning, I was just an innocent—looking for love. Then things got out of hand. It all began when I was about ten years old and started falling in love.

My first crush was on a boy named Alan. Oh, how I loved him. I just knew he was going to make all my dreams come true.

Alan was embarrassed and angry that I liked him so much. He told me not to write his name on my school books. He threw rocks at me when I walked by his house. I can still feel the sting of those missiles. I cried and was humiliated, but nothing discouraged me.

Every day I watched Alan play baseball at the park. At school, during recess, I would sneak into the cloakroom and put on Alan's jacket. I wanted to touch something that was his—I wanted to smell his presence. I also wrote in my diary about my love for Alan. Day after day, I described the bittersweet pain of unrequited love, hoping that someday Alan would love me too.

There were other infatuations over the years. The pattern was always the same. I fell in love and believed that only this particular boy could make me happy. And I always felt so powerless - as if I couldn't help myself.

Eventually, I would get emotionally and physically sick from yearning to be with someone I could not have. Then, when the pain became unbearable, the obsession faded and I found someone more promising to adore from a distance.

High school was not a happy time for me. I prayed that someone would ask me out for a date. One time I did get a call from a boy. He asked me out and I agreed to go. I was so excited and nervous that I stayed up all night making a new dress.

The next day at school some boys snickered at me as I walked by, and that night someone called to tell me that the phone call I had gotten the night before was just a joke. I was so embarrassed, I wanted to die.

When I was nineteen years old, I became desperate to have a relationship. I wanted to have a boyfriend and I was willing to do anything to get one. Of course, I did not feel loveable enough to attract someone I really liked, and I was too impatient to wait for someone compatible to come along, so I got involved with the first person who showed any interest in me.

I met Ray (not his real name) walking down the street in San Francisco. I was visiting the Haight Asbury district made famous by the hippies. Ray was 25 years old, unemployed, and living with his mother. I started spending a lot of time with Ray and within a few months, I was pregnant. I decided to sign up for government assistance (welfare) and find a place where Ray and I could live together. From that point on, I became Ray's caretaker. I paid the bills, bought Ray's clothes and gave him money for drugs.

I accepted a lot of neglect from Ray. I seemed to have a high tolerance for suffering because in my mind this was the price I had to pay for having a man in my life. Ray took advantage of this. He only came home when he felt like it. He didn't give me any affection.

Ray and I didn't even talk very much, unless he was telling me what to do. He also took all of my money, except what went to pay the bills. Sometimes I would try to hide money for a rainy day. Then Ray would get into some kind of trouble with gambling or drugs and beg me to give him some money. He said the men he owed money to would kill him if he did not pay up. I can still see him standing there, tears running down his face, asking me to save his life. Of course, I always gave in. I felt responsible for Ray.

I also accepted a lot of dishonesty from Ray. I had no idea what it felt like to trust him. Usually he lied to me about other women. He said he was not having affairs and he usually was. Deep down I knew what was going on, but I buried my head in the sand because I was afraid if I said something to Ray, he might leave me.

Of course, I wanted more than I was getting out of the relationship. I was just too afraid to demand it. So I just cried when my birthday went unnoticed. When Ray didn't come home at night, I spent hours lying in the bed, curled up like a child, waiting for his car to pull up.

Despite my dependency on this relationship, I tried several times to end it. I remember after six months of being with Ray, I wanted to leave him. When I told him I was going to leave, he got very sad. He said, "I guess you've gotten what you want and now you're ready to move on and leave me behind." I felt guilty when Ray said this and I stayed with him to keep from hurting his feelings. I projected my fear of being abandoned on to him and assumed that he could not survive if I left him.

Later in the relationship, I thought about leaving Ray again, but I felt guilty about withdrawing my financial support. I knew Ray had become dependent on me. I was also afraid to leave the relationship because I knew it meant facing my fear of loneliness and giving up my identity as a caretaker. Most of all, I didn't want to face the emotional pain of breaking up so I just kept putting it off, hoping my misery would end someday.

Another time I asked Ray to leave, but when he started packing his bags, I panicked. The next thing I knew, I was begging Ray to stay—like a child begging her mother not to leave her alone in the dark. During this scene, my fear of abandonment overwhelmed me and I was ready to do anything to avoid feeling the panic that gripped my heart.

While it seemed as if I would never leave, eventually I did fall in love with someone else and decided to ask Ray for a divorce. Unfortunately, Ray was not ready to lose me. When I told him I was going to leave, he held a knife to my throat and threatened to kill me. Then he beat me up and held me prisoner in the house.

Ray kept saying to me, "I know you still love me, just admit it." After three days of this, I agreed to stay with Ray and he immediately calmed down. Then I said, "Ray, it's time to cook dinner and I need to go to the store and get some things." Ray agreed to let me go and I quickly hurried out of the door. Once I was safe, I went to a phone booth and called the police. Ray was told by the police to leave the house and he did.

The first man I got involved with after Ray was not much better and that relationship failed too. From this point on, I became involved in a series of short-term relationships similar to the one I had with Ray. All of these relationships failed because I was too emotionally unstable to select an appropriate partner; and even if I did, I couldn't sustain a relationship because of my neediness, low self-esteem, and fear of abandonment. So as the years passed, my hungry heart went unsatisfied and this made me even more desperate to find love.

It was during these years of endless searching for love that I neglected my children. Kaitland and Randy [not their real names] were always important to me in between relationships. I cooked their meals, washed their clothes, walked them to school, volunteered as a PTA mother, went to their sports events, and tucked them in at nights. But when I had a boyfriend, things changed. I am ashamed to admit this, but I actually brought men I barely knew into the house to stay for long periods and while these men were there, they became more important than my children.

Eventually, all these toxic relationships and my guilt about neglecting my children, took its toll and my health began to deteriorate. I developed a spastic colon and high blood pressure. I was chronically depressed and almost died in two car accidents. Once I couldn't see the road because I was crying and the other time I was fantasizing instead of looking where I was going. Finally, after another failed relationship, I was in so much pain I swallowed a bottle of aspirin.

My father died in 1982. The day before, I had asked my boyfriend if I could use the car to visit my father. My boyfriend said "no" so I didn't go, and of course my father died. I cried about this in front of my boyfriend and he promptly punched me in the eye. I guess he thought I was trying to make him feel guilty. So I sat at my father's funeral with a black eye wondering what had become of my life.

On the day of my father's funeral, I went to work. I wanted to be a "brave little soldier." Across from me was the desk of a co-worker by the name of Barry. Barry had only recently been assigned to the desk near me after the office manager, for no logical reason, decided to move everybody around to a new location.

Around 4:00 in the afternoon I was typing away when I looked up to see Barry staring at me. I was curious about this and decided that it meant he cared about my situation—perhaps he felt sorry for me. This was good news for someone who felt invisible and unloved. I would take any kind of attention that I could get.

I started stopping by Barry's office more often after this. It did not take long for me to fall in love. Eventually I asked Barry if he wanted to go out on a date. He very nicely said he was dating someone else. I was devastated, but undeterred.

I decided at that moment that I would seduce him— come hell or high water. Thus, in the blink of an eye, my final toxic relationship began—the last one before finding my way into a new life.

My master plan to seduce Barry was to lose weight and become so attractive that Barry could not resist me. Men were basically weak, I assumed, when it came to sex. Over the next few months, I took off a lot of weight and spent all of my money on sexy clothes. Unfortunately, my plan didn't work. Barry was my friend and that was all.

To his credit, Barry never gave into my obsession to be with him. Instead, he only tried to help me with my depression. He never once mentioned the heavy drinking which had become alcoholic by this time or the dieting which had gotten out of control.

One day I was sitting in Barry's office, very depressed, and suddenly I started crying. I turned to Barry and said, "Barry, can you die of loneliness?" I really thought he was going to tell me to stop feeling sorry for myself, but instead he looked at me with such compassion and then he turned and said to me, "Yes, you can die of loneliness. I know this first hand."

I looked at him astonished, because after months of pouring out my heart to him, he had never once told me anything personal about himself. Finally, after a long pause, he said, "Susan, I think you need to go somewhere where people understand you." That was it. No warnings about my alcoholic drinking or obsessive dieting—just a simple "get help."

I didn't visit Barry for a few days after this. When I did see him, he asked me if I had gotten any help. I looked at him and blurted out, "No, I am afraid they might cure me." I was surprised at what I had said. Barry just laughed. It was only years later that I realized I had become addicted to the pain - the depression, the self pity, the misery. It was the only thread I had left and I was afraid to let it go. The idea of happiness made me nervous.

Eventually, I did get help. I went to a support group. At first, I really didn't think my behavior was out of control, but as the facilitator explained how the program worked, something she said caught my attention. "You will have to learn how to ask for help," she announced. "Not me," I said to myself with the assurance of a lonely, stubborn survivor. "I can take care of myself."

I had been attending the support group for about a year when Robin Norwood released her book "Women Who Love Too Much." Needless to say, I recognized many of my own obsessive behavior patterns in the book. Enthusiastically, I looked around for a "Women Who Love Too Much" support group. Unfortunately, there were none in my area. Undaunted, I started my own meeting for women who wanted to deal with the issues introduced by Robin Norwood. This seemed like a great way to promote my own recovery and at the same time, offer other women the opportunity to turn their lives around.

A year after the group began, when I was about a mile down the road to recovery (according to Robin Norwood's chart), I became interested in teaching others about the "disease" of "loving too much." Armed with a teaching credential, a desire to be instrumental in helping others, and the support of all my friends, I approached the principal of a local adult school. He was very enthusiastic about the general subject matter of the course I wanted to teach, but he encouraged me to allow men in my class.

Excited about the challenge of teaching, I set aside Robin Norwood's book for awhile and began reading other literature about obsessive behavior in relationships. This, of course, was a great learning experience for me. I was amazed to find out how much had been written about love, obsession, and dependency. (Even Kierkergaard, as far back as the 1840s, wrote about the "habitual" nature of romantic love. See *Works of Love*.)

Once I had acquired a lot of professional information about love and addiction (information which I could use to supplement what I had learned from my own personal experiences and the experiences of the women in my support group), I began to prepare an outline for my course. My goal was to condense and clarify many of the ideas introduced by others, and then to interject some of my own concepts. By my own concepts, I mean an analysis of my own experiences.

When I finally had what I thought was a model of a course about love addiction, I taught my first class. It was an exhilarating experience, and the response of my students really made it clear that I had put together some valuable information about a very serious problem.

Today, I am still involved in helping other love addicts. In 2006 I celebrated 24 years of recovery. I am happier than I have ever been and enjoy helping others find their own recovery.

Well, this is my story. As I said, I am a survivor of a painful disorder. And while I might be embarrassed about some of the things I did in the name of love, I am proud of how far I have come in the last 24 years. If you also suffer from love addiction, I hope my story inspires you to change and reach out for a brighter tomorrow.

A Safe Place

In August I came to LAA in tears, only hours after breaking off a four year relationship with a Person of Addiction (Qualifier). During my entire 30 years of marriage, I had Qualifiers on the side off and on. They were mostly intense emotional connections.

As the disease progressed, it moved into the physical realm to a small degree. I never slept with any Qualifier. That was not what it was about. It was about emotions, intimacy, and closeness. Those aren't bad things, but the type I am referring to is the delusional kind filled with illusion and fantasy. My ability to tell what was real and what was not real was greatly diminished.

After ending my relationship with my last Qualifier, I found this site and started posting and reading. It saved me. It helped me so much to know I wasn't alone. There were certain individuals on this site, in particular, that had a lifesaving influence on me. I will be eternally grateful. And I will always consider them friends. As I went through the 12 steps, I spent a lot of time on each question and pondered. My step sponsor was terrific.

Over time the obsessions became less. Soon I no longer had any feelings for my Qualifier. My relationship with my wife improved tremendously. I was able to talk openly with her about my past. There is nothing in my life right now that she doesn't know. And it brings peace to my soul. I have worked my way through the steps at least one time now. The confession part was the most humbling, but paid the biggest dividends. Now I am ready to serve others.

During recovery I have been tested several times. I may start to fall into a trap but my awareness now allows me to know how to turn off the obsessive impulses. Yes, I can have a regular life now, with friends of all kinds, men and women, and be able to see things the way they really are. I know how to put up boundaries and yet be able to share my innermost feelings with others through music and word. I do realize however, that some of you might not be in the same safe place.

And most of all, I know who I am now. I am a son of God. A being of light. I am a husband and a father. I no longer need to sludge around in the darkness of illusion, fantasy, anxiety and pain.

Those are things I have left behind. But only a constant awareness and remembering who I am will keep them at bay.

Recovery is possible. Everyone must know that. The concept of recovery is not just another fantasy. It is real. And it is something that you can achieve. Now is the time to stop judging people by what they have been in the past. Instead, celebrate their deliverance out of the abyss of obsession and compulsive behavior. A love addict can again see the light of reality, peace, and true love. When I look at my wife now, I see my eternal companion. There is no one else. If someone else feels I'm into them right now, they are living a fantasy! This recovery has changed my life. It will never be the same. And the names of all those on this site who have helped me along the way will be branded on my soul forever. I do consider you ALL my friends, regardless of what you think of me.

My wife is the love of my life. My family is precious to me. God is guiding me now.

Now my next goal is to do things that I have procrastinated doing in the past because of my disease. I need to put aside my self doubt. I believe in myself now. I can stop being afraid to share my music. I've written so much music. A lot of it I've only shared with my wife and a few close friends. I didn't trust anyone else. That was always a frightening leap of faith for me. It needs to come out of my dresser drawer and be shared. There is some music I have published and I have performed a lot. But it is only a fraction of what I could have achieved. I have always been afraid. So I need to stop being afraid to reach out to other creative people. My wife has always encouraged me to do so. And I need to not be afraid to take on the risk of a big project (like a movie score). I could have accomplished so much more if I had not had this affliction. I didn't have any self confidence. Now I know who I am. And I'm going to reach out. Ending the love addiction is only the start. Now is the time to do all the things that a complete person does.

A Sense of Belonging

I was raised by alcoholic parents, the youngest of three children. By the time I came along, my mother was done with little babies and so my early years were spent, at best, in benign neglect and, at worst, in outright abuse—both physical and emotional. My father was in recovery but he was a dry drunk—his behavior was alcoholic but he didn't drink anymore. We were the model family on the outside—wealthy, belonged to the country club, I was a champion swimmer, my sister played team tennis and my brother was a gifted musician. To the outside world we had it all, but inside our home, it was like a roller coaster of calm and explosion. My parents' angry outbursts were completely unpredictable and I learned at a very early age to be pleasing and quiet in order to avoid their wrath. Additionally, I learned that I was unlovable, unable to make a good decision for myself, worthless and insignificant. God forbid anyone ever talk about feelings in my house.

When I was 15, my mother died of lung cancer. This was both a blessing and a curse for me. The abuse and confusion of living with her active alcoholism were gone but my father chose to abdicate any role as a parent he had ever attempted; I found myself sitting down with him while he told me to forget my mother and then he left. My brother and sister were away at college so there I was in this great big house, plenty of money on the kitchen table every morning, plenty of food in the cupboards and a car but I actually only saw my father a half dozen times in the next four years.

I got myself into a good college, I spent time with my friends and their mothers took pity on me and taught me to drive and to cook; I was "the rock." No one could believe how well I was faring with the loss of both of my parents at the same time. I went away to college and in the middle of my freshman year, I met the man who would become my first husband. I believed him to be the love of my life. I gave up everything for him: my grades, my friends, and my identity. I spent all of my time with him and with his family and was happier than I had ever been in my life.

My husband began cheating on me with other women after about six months of dating, but I ignored it, made excuses, and stuck with him. He graduated my freshman year and moved to the other side of the country. I still held out that we would be together, allowing him to waltz in and out of my life at will for the next year. When we weren't together, I felt a physical pain like no other. A despair in my heart and in my head that cut to my soul. I knew this man was my destiny and I was willing to do anything to be able to ride off into the sunset with him and live happily ever after.

He continued to cheat on me and at the advice of my friends, I ended it with him. I spent my junior year in rebellion. I drank too much, I slept around too much and I found myself in endless pursuit of any man who would medicate my feelings of worthlessness and pain.

At the end of the year, my ex was in town for a track meet and he swept me off my feet with a marriage proposal. I believed it to be the Hollywood ending I was searching for so I, of course, said yes. We were married and moved to the other side of the country so that he could train for the Olympic decathlon.

It didn't matter to me that he didn't have the raw physical talent for this. I was going to support him no matter what. It didn't matter that I didn't want to live 3000 miles from everything I had ever known and it didn't matter to me that I was one semester away from finishing my college degree—I decided to leave and marry him instead. The only thing that mattered to me was that this man was going to complete me. I spent the next five years disappearing. Every shred of identity that I had went away. I worked to support us, he couldn't hold a job, I was his cheerleader for his Olympic dream and when he came home out of the blue one day to tell me he was going to fly jets for the Navy and we were moving to Florida, I supported him gladly in that as well. He continued to lie and cheat and I continued to ignore it. The only thing that mattered was that he was in my life.

We moved to Florida for officer training and flight school and then were stationed in Virginia Beach. I had gotten into mortgage lending by default as a result of a temporary job and decided it was worth staying in. My degree was going to be in teaching, I had dreams of being a college English professor, but that didn't fit my husband's plan so I ignored my own dreams and did what he needed.

We had only just arrived in Virginia Beach when a friend of his came to stay with us for a couple of months. I "fell in love" with this man and separated from my husband so that we could be together. This one was the opposite of my first husband. He was steady and reliable, he thought I was amazing, he told me how badly I was being treated by my husband and he told me I deserved better. I divorced the first one and married the second one that year and in doing so, I transferred all of my illusions about my first husband to my second.

It turned out he was exactly like my first husband. He was more subtle and manipulative about it but he actually didn't care if I was happy. He wanted me to take care of him. My opinions didn't matter, I was never able to convince him to do anything in the manner that I wanted and he cheated on me. We spent the next twelve years together and had two daughters.

For some reason,I was never able to see my responsibility in any of this. I only saw how badly I was being treated and fantasized constantly about other men, how great it would be with whoever the object of my obsession currently was, and how deeply it was my husband's fault that I was so miserable. Yet I could never find the strength to leave and anytime it looked like it was a possibility, I clung to him harder than ever before.

My husband, who had also been in the Navy, got out and was not able to hold a job. I again supported us while he pursued his dreams of being a day trader, managing funds, publishing a newsletter—whatever he wanted. None of it ever panned out.

I went in to therapy during this time and my therapist mentioned a book to me called "Women Who Love Too Much." He told me that he thought I might be a love addict. It was a fairly new concept at the time and I ignored it completely. The problem was obviously the men in my life, that they didn't appreciate me and that I just hadn't found the right one yet.

I had an affair with a business partner when my husband was having an affair with someone he worked with and we separated for about seven months. We went back and forth in trying to work it out for a few years after that and finally divorced. I dated voraciously for about two years including dating my most recent ex-husband. I was engaged twice and in endless pursuit of the "One." The hole in my soul was deep and scary and I would do whatever it took to fill it. It was a time of obsession and denial for me. In the grocery store one day, a man introduced himself to me who I found to be amazingly handsome. He told me he had seen me at professional meetings in town and that he had wanted to find a way to meet me. I had stayed in mortgage lending as I could always find a job in it and it paid well enough to get us through the times when my husband had not been working. This man was in the same industry and he was an alcoholic in recovery.

At the time, I thought it was a match made in heaven and so did he. He asked me to marry him after two weeks, moved in after three months and we were married three months after that. I kicked him out the first time another three months later. As long as my kids were home, we were able to maintain a sense of peace but when they were at their dad's, life would explode in the exact unpredictable manner it had when I was a child.

My third husband's anger was abusive and downright mean but I had just enough therapy under my belt to be a lot stronger than I had in my previous two marriages. I continued in therapy and he and I separated and got back together a dozen times in the next five years. I had risen in the ranks of my company and was offered a huge promotion in another state. It happened to be his home state and hometown so together we decided to go for it.

I was on the train getting ready to return from my house hunting trip in the new city when he called me on my cell phone and told me that he wasn't coming with me. He said that he didn't support the move or the promotion and that he had taken a large chunk of money out of my bank account by finding a blank check and writing it to himself. I made the move, we separated and the beginning of the end came for me.

I had spent the past 23 years making all of my decisions based on my addiction to men. My teenage daughter had moved more than once a year her entire life. I had worked at a dozen different companies.

We had spent the past eight years in the same town and it felt like home but the houses and the men kept rotating. I went ahead and moved to the next location where I spent the next two and half years in absolute active addict mode. I refused to recognize my behavior and spent my time excusing my husband's behavior and taking him back, dating relentlessly through online dating sites when we were not together and doing whatever it took to medicate the emptiness and unworthiness I felt.

During this time, my life was an amazing dichotomy—my career was on fire and I was very successful on a national level at a huge mortgage company. I was promoted three times in two and a half years. I was making the best female friends that I had had since college and yet I was unhappier than I had ever been.

Through an online dating site, I met a man and dated him for about two months. He was completely emotionally unavailable and had a very angry streak so I had ended it. My husband and I then tried again and when finally, I decided that I had nothing left to give, we divorced.

I had just received a promotion at work and had met a new man on the online site. I dated this man for four months in the most intensely addictive manner. I took time away from work to talk on the phone and text message him, we talked far in to the night almost every day, I ignored my daughters, my own responsibilities, including financial ones, and every red flag that was going off in my head.

He had violated my trust almost from the first day but said he loved me and was in love for the first time in his life. His professional life was stressful and that was why he made some of the decisions that he made. Whatever his excuse, I accepted it and stayed with him. Finally he came clean and told me he was an internet porn addict, and that he wanted me to go that direction with him. My answer, amazingly, was that he had to choose between that and me. He chose the porn.

I was reeling from the pain and emptiness I was feeling, my job was beginning to unravel at work, my daughters were not doing well, my finances were a mess so what did I do? I emailed the man I had dated for a couple of months the year before, the one who was emotionally unavailable and angry and I spent the next ten months in hell. I was abused emotionally and physically, I was ignored, belittled, treated as if I didn't matter and I accepted this.

I stayed with him, hanging on by my teeth and convincing myself that this man was the love of my life and we were meant to be together. He would manipulate me with anger and withdrawal and when he was withdrawing and I couldn't find him, I would leave my children asleep in bed and drive to his house in the middle of the night to make sure he was okay.

This man was manic depressive and I convinced myself that the up times made the down times okay. He refused to ever make plans with me so I would drop everything if it meant spending a bit of time with him because I never knew when the next opportunity would be.

I woke up each morning thinking about whether or not it was going to be a good day or a bad day with him. I ignored my children and their needs, I ignored my bill and I did the bare minimum at work to get by. I obsessed constantly about this man and I lost my self completely. Any connection I had ever had to a Higher Power was gone.

My friends were tired of my constant conversation about how it was or was not going with this man. My life was empty and meaningless and yet I clung to my "boyfriend" because I knew he was the only one capable of making me feel better. I nagged constantly, got angry with him, he screamed at me and threw things; he bruised me and yet I stayed in it - until the day he ended it.

I drove home from his house after 19 hours of crying, screaming, abuse and degradation and decided that I was going to kill myself. I had a beautiful scenario in my head where I would get into his bed, wearing his favorite underwear and when he walked through the doorway I would have his gun in my mouth. I would point it upwards and shoot. I couldn't wait for my brains to be splattered all over his headboard.

That was when something in me snapped—but in the right way. I started thinking about things my third husband had said to me about his alcoholism. How his addict would do anything in order to get the next drink. How his addict would compromise everything that was important to him in order to survive. I looked back at the past 29 years and realized that my behaviors in regards to men were a mirror of those words. And I remembered that therapist long ago who told me that there was an addiction to love.

I went home and googled Love Addicts Anonymous (LAA). I was astounded. I sat at the computer crying as I read the stories of so many people who felt exactly the way I did. People who couldn't breathe if they were not in a relationship, people who felt no sense of worth, no sense of belonging to anyone or anything outside of being in a romantic relationship.

I called my therapist and made an immediate appointment. I spent four days in intensive treatment. I read two books in one day. I realized the depths of my addiction and that those choices had been mine. I claimed responsibility for my part in the mess that my life had become and I vowed to change.

Today, I live in the town that I spent eight years in and feel at home again. I left the big job and took a lower stress one and I am now there for my daughters. I attend LAA online and Al-Anon in face to face meetings. I go to church. The recognition that my life was completely out of control has set me free. I now talk to my Higher Power sometimes moment to moment. And He answers me every single time. Now I experience the joy of the most simple things in life. I treasure the quiet and lack of drama. I know and like myself. I have learned to take care of myself and my deepest needs - the need to be cherished, to be unconditionally loved and the need for that sense of belonging. I've learned about the power of forgiveness - of my parents, of the men in my life, and of myself. I have learned to work the 12 Steps continually and especially on those days when my addict peeks her head around the corner and wants some attention, I turn it over to the care of the God of my understanding and He takes the pain away every single time. As I meet men who are interested in me, I am now able to make healthy choices in regards to them based on my needs and those of my daughters and the values that I have.

I like to visualize two things: one is my heart. I look at it and it is a little bloody, there's barbed wire sticking out of it in places, it has scabs, but it is still beating strong and true and I can see that the wounds are healing. I picture it in my hands and I am giving it to God. He takes it from me and He heals it. My heart belongs to Him now and I know He will take good care of it as He teaches me how to make healthy decisions for myself.

The second thing I do when I get lonely is to again picture my Higher Power. He is huge and gentle and His arms are wrapped around me. There is a breeze and it smells good, like sandalwood and peppermint…and I am safe and I know that I have always belonged to Him and that I am not alone.

I was Powerless

I am 37 years old and I have been responsible for taking care of someone else my entire life. My parents came from dysfunctional, addicted, violent homes and were unable to break the cycle. They did the best they knew how but my parents were troubled and unable to model a healthy relationship. I became their source of happiness.

I was also my mother's confidante and surrogate partner/parent as well as my father's surrogate partner/parent. It was total enmeshment. I was responsible for keeping them happy, keeping them healthy and making them feel safe and secure.

I felt special and loved, but in reality I was abandoned. As my caretakers, it was their responsibility to take care of me and attempt to provide for my emotional needs, but the reality was that I was taking care of them to meet their emotional needs. I quickly learned that my primary job was to take care of my parents, yet it was impossible for me to meet their needs because as a child I was incapable.

I did not know this as a child and it instilled a sense of failure and inadequacy in me. This in turn made me feel that I was unimportant and had no worth. I felt responsible for others, accepted blame readily, was eager to please, deferred to other's opinions, and feared being considered selfish if I acted assertively. I quickly learned that I should be a "good, happy girl." I remember crying and my parents telling me to please stop because it was upsetting them. I learned that my anger and sadness were bad emotions that upset people so I never expressed them. Instead I felt anxiety, fear and somatic paining, I exuded happiness.

I had so buried any other emotions that I truly did not know how they felt. My feelings were a source of discomfort and this discomfort made me unable to develop trust in my own feelings and judgments. Anxiety, fear and chaos were familiar feelings for me and therefore comfortable. I thrived on these feelings. I sought these feelings out because they made me feel normal.

I have scattered memories of my childhood. I have happy memories but many of my memories involve fearful situations. There are also memories of the various boys that I have obsessed about since I was four years old. They were boys I went to school with or boys in the neighborhood. Sometimes I wouldn't even know the boy; I would only know his name. I would create personas for these boys and I would create our fantasy life. I would carry a torch for some of these boys for years.

My first real relationship began when I was in high school and ended when he pulled a gun on me at college. After that relationship, I no longer picked violent men but I continued to pick unsafe men. I never experienced withdrawal for very long because I rolled from one relationship into another. I would meet a guy and we would have this amazing connection.

We would feel immediately comfortable and attached to each other and spend every second possible together. It was like we had known each other our entire lives. That was the great high. The reality is I have known "this guy" my entire life because he is always the same guy, just a different name and face. I would give up all other aspects of my life to spend time with "him."

I did not know or understand the importance of balance in my life. Our relationship would be great for a period of time and then the magic and the high would start to wear off. I would start to see him as he really was instead of who I had created him to be. I would mold myself into the person that I thought "he" wanted me to be. I was very attuned as to how to behave to make others comfortable and happy.

I feared abandonment from him but did not realize I was abandoning myself. We fed off each other's unhealthy behaviors and became completely enmeshed with each other. I had no identity. I didn't know what I wanted, what I liked, and what I didn't like. I learned to like what "he" liked and want what "he" wanted.

Eventually, the high would be gone and I would feel really bad about myself. I would also feel completely suffocated and smothered by him. I would feel disgusted, unlovable, and worth nothing. This would lead me to act out to get those good feelings again.

I would begin intrigue and then become involved in an emotional affair. Once the emotional connection was established with someone else, I felt safe to leave the current relationship. I didn't have to deal with abandonment because I had replaced one guy with another. And I was again on the high because I had really found "the one" this time.

When I was in junior high I realized that I had the ability to seduce. As I got older, I used seduction and sex as tools to manipulate and feel powerful. When I felt powerful, I felt self worth. However, I did not enjoy sex. Sex was meant to make "him" feel good. When I was able to make him feel good, I felt powerful. I was incapable of being vulnerable.

In my mind, power and vulnerability could not coexist. In addition, I had an overwhelming fear of intimacy and commitment. I had never learned to trust and I DID NOT trust. I had erected great walls to barricade myself for protection. Intimacy and commitment meant enmeshment, suffocation, smothering. It meant being responsible for another person's care and happiness. In essence I felt responsible for their life. It terrified me. I did not want the responsibility of someone else. I only wanted to be responsible for myself but I couldn't even do that. I was not taking care of myself because I never learned how. I had only learned to take care of others. But my actions had hurt a lot of people and affected some friendships. I was putting myself into unsafe situations and I was creating a considerable amount of stress for myself.

There are two events that brought me into therapy and Love Addicts Anonymous (LAA). The first was that I became engaged to a gay man. We were both in denial about his sexuality but deep down, we both knew.

I was obsessed with him and with getting him to admit that he was gay. If he would admit he was gay, then it wasn't me. But he was in deep denial. He never admitted it and that made me feel like something was wrong with me. I wasn't good enough, I wasn't pretty enough, I wasn't smart enough, I wasn't funny enough, I wasn't desirable enough and I absolutely was not lovable enough. I was WORTH NOTHING.

He finally decided to move out of our house and out of the state. It took him two months to leave and it was the most painful withdrawal that I have ever experienced. I fell into depression, suffered from insomnia and was riddled with painful shingles. It was time to seek help. I went into therapy. The problem I had with therapy was that I was dishonest. I did not give my therapist all of the information. I was not going to recover. Two months into therapy I found another man to get involved with. He was amazing—everything I had dreamed of.

I stopped going to therapy and a year later we got engaged. I was the happiest person alive. The panic, anxiety and feelings of suffocation all started when I began to plan the wedding. I relieved my fear and anxiety as I always had—I acted out. I began an affair with my married boss. I ended my engagement. I entered into one of the most chaotic and stressful years of my life.

What finally turned my life around was admitting that I had a problem that I could not control. I was powerless. I turned to God and prayer. I have always known God, even as a child. I accepted God into my life when I was nine years old. I turned to God throughout my life. However, when I was acting out I turned away from God. I am so thankful for His grace, patience and forgiveness. During this stressful time, I prayed. Through prayer, I found a new therapist. I made a commitment to be honest with her and I was. After three months of extensive therapy, she recommended two 12 step programs for me. Those programs were CoDA and LAA. I began these programs in March 2006.

Through therapy I was able to acknowledge and accept how my childhood abandonment issues affected my behavior. Family of origin and inner child work helped me to discover that I had very little self worth and no idea what a boundary was. I did not feel worthy of being loved. I accepted bad, unhealthy, dysfunctional and unsafe relationships because that is what I felt I was worth.

Through therapy and this program I am slowly learning who I am. I have learned to get in touch with and recognize all of my emotions. I realize that jolt of adrenaline that I once considered exciting is not exciting, but a warning. I recognize when I am beginning to fantasize and stop myself. I recognize when I am about to engage in intrigue and I stop myself. I say a prayer and thank God for helping me to recognize what I am doing.

I still struggle daily. Some of my struggles include: learning to communicate instead of withdraw, learning what healthy sex is, allowing myself to be vulnerable and intimate, learning to trust, and not allowing others to define who I am. Thankfully, I am being honest with myself and taking care of myself. Most importantly I am no longer getting my worth from others. I am not relying on other people to make me feel good. I now know how to get worth for myself by meeting my needs and when I meet my needs every day, I feel good. I now understand what my eight needs are and I have the tools to meet these needs daily, thanks to my therapist. Other tools that I have found to be helpful in my journey toward recovery are Therapy, Meetings, Reading and Researching, Journaling, Prayer and Learning to parent myself.

With all of these tools and God, I know that I am a valuable and worthy person and that a happy life is possible for me.

Mountain Climbing

I don't believe there was ever a time that I wasn't in love. How embarrassing, but it started with some pretty serious fantasies about "Captain Kirk" when I was 7 or 8 years old. The young, sexy Captain Kirk, that is, with his tight black pants and blond hair. I was painfully in love with him. And I can still remember my father humoring me, telling me, "let's call him on the phone right now…" and actually getting one of his friends to pretend to be the real William Shatner.

Right as I was on the brink of actualizing my love and hearing his voice, my mother stepped in and said, "Stop teasing her." I can still see my dad laughing at the top of the stairs with the phone in his hand, because he thought it was so funny that he'd tricked me.

I don't believe I was ever physically abused, and yet at a very young age (about 5) I found my father's pornography magazines everywhere and was very possibly sexually abused by him a time or two when I was older (8 or 9) under the guise of being punished.

As for my father himself—he was a psychopathic, narcissistic, manic-depressive, alcoholic, pill popping, gambler & sex addict. Not to mention a professional con artist and white-collar criminal. My mother, for 20 years at least, supported and loved him in a rather submissive. I have no identity of my own.

I lost myself in men. In high school it was all about sex. And well into my 20s it was about love and sex. My relationships (to me) were deep and some meaningful. But mostly one of two things occurred: I either chose men who made me feel completely in love but neglected me, or I chose men who loved and adored me, but whom I neglected and ran away from. There was never any balance.

Eventually, I met and married a sex/porn/computer addict who ignored me (physically, mentally and emotionally) and abused me, raped me, cheated on me often during my second pregnancy and eventually blamed me for leaving him and ruining his life. And yet, comforting to me was the fact that he was unable to express any real emotions.

The one underlying theme through all of my relationships is—that I left them all. I bailed out. I moved on.

After my divorce, I was scared to death of marriage and commitment AND sex. But I so desperately wanted LOVE.

Enter George

My most recent and long-term boyfriend of three years was a Seductive Withholder and Avoidant. When I met him he was quite lonely, as was I. Though I can't say that he ever "came on strong" sexually, he was a flirt, did pursue me and was definitely interested in me. Our sex life was wonderful for the first eight months. In fact, our whole relationship, up to the one year mark, was like a fantasy. He was sexy, loving, a great communicator, hard working, very interested in me, and very giving. But suddenly, as if we had crossed an imaginary line, it all changed.

He began withholding all forms of intimacy from me the following year, giving me every excuse in the book to avoid sex (prostate problems, "I love you TOO much to do that to you," "I'm afraid of STDs," and so on). Not only did he withhold sex, but also general forms of emotional tenderness as well. He never touched me, kissed me or made any advances whatsoever. And he stopped sleeping over because my "bed was too soft," or he didn't feel comfortable in my house, in my neighborhood, etc. I liked to sleep with the windows open in the spring and he couldn't handle that. We did hold hands a lot and hug when we saw each other. But in my mind, it became more of a brother-sister type relationship than a romantic one between a man and a woman.

And yet I stayed. We broke up at least seven times over the next couple years, but would get back together, every time repeating the same pattern: sex, love and passion during the first month or so and then a slow decay of emotion and pulling away on his part (fear of commitment, withdrawal and avoidance) and a building of anger, resentment and frustration on my part.

I suppose because I was no longer under such obvious abuse (as when I was married), I considered my relationship with George to be normal and healthy. George and I were, after all, best friends and aside from withholding sex from me, he did not withhold love—or so I thought.

He was very "into" me. He called every day, we spent LOADS of time together, we were extremely compatible, into the same things, and treated me with as much respect as I had ever known. He never cheated, wasn't a liar and at times, was very giving. And most importantly, I was attracted to him

All that aside, he had debilitating issues that went completely against my value system and yet I chose him over my values. He smoked pot, had no libido, didn't take care of his appearance and avoided intimacy like the plague. There was no next step with him. There would be no marriage, no moving in, and no increased intimacy. I was at the end of the road.

I stayed as long as I did because I believed I had to make compromises and that I couldn't "have it all." And that aside from these issues, we shared a great life together. Surely we all have to make sacrifices, don't we? Especially if we feel love towards someone?

And yet, underneath it all, I knew something was wrong. I wasn't being true to myself. After a year of no sex with George, an affair with a guy I never loved (to fill the void that George left) and about five months of going back and forth between the both of them, I hit bottom. I thought I had done so well for myself in avoiding someone like my ex-husband, but in actuality, I only went to the opposite extreme. One was a sex addict, the other a sexual anorexic. I was somewhere in between.

That's when I found Love Addicts Anonymous (LAA) and simultaneously got into a support group for another of my addictions—cigarettes. I suppose because I had viewed myself as a victim of my father's addictive behavior for so long, it was unreal to think that I could be an addict myself. And when I began the step work for LAA and saw with my very own eyes how my life had become unmanageable and how I was really addicted to men (because for the first time EVER I wrote it all down on paper!), it occurred to me that I had a serious, life-threatening problem.

I had given up goals, given up direction, given up my dreams and plans, all for the "hope" of a new man. I had wasted HOURS, DAYS, WEEKS and YEARS on thinking, or rather obsessing of nothing but my relationship to whomever. I had let men control me. I had spent EXORBITANT amounts of money on men because I either felt sorry for them, wanted to impress them, or secretly wanted to buy their love.

I had spent EXORBITANT amounts of money on men just to visit them in foreign countries or call them on the phone and chat for hours. I had embarrassed myself, accepted the unacceptable and abandoned my VALUES for men. I had even once or twice put my children at risk of emotional hurt or damage, isolated myself from my family, lowered my standards and done things I would not normally do, just for a man. I had ignored my children and I had ignored my opportunity for true growth.

It was time to change, so I found Love Addicts Anonymous.

Several things occurred to me during this time of what I like to refer to as my "enlightenment."

I realized that my ex was a representation of my father. At first, I resisted this. I had heard this spoken so many times and I could see some of their similarities but I wasn't convinced on any deep level that I was "dating" my dad. Then it occurred to me. My love for George was one sided. I really adored him. His personality was wonderful, he was funny, hard-working, a musician, grungy, and we had a lot in common. I was so darn happy to be with someone that I actually LIKED that I never took into account how he treated me.

I never considered that his love for me was also a part of the equation. He neglected me, basically, and it was pretty painful. I allowed it to happen because the thrill of being with someone FUN and ALIVE was more important than meeting my own needs to be loved and treated well. Did it matter that he loved me? No. What mattered then was that I loved him.

Through that, I saw the parallel. I adored my father. I loved his personality. He was funny, hard-working, a musician...we had a lot in common. I felt

ALIVE with my father because of who he was as a person. And YET, as per my mother's advice, I was told to love him "as is" and not take into account how he treated me. It's no surprise to know that he treated me much the same as George: neglectful, uncaring, and he always had something more important to do than spend time with me.

The important part was this: to love my father and not get anything in return is OK for a father/daughter relationship. I cannot change my father (I can't go out and get another one) and therefore, I have to accept him for who he is, especially if I like him and want to hang out with him. But this type of relationship is NOT OK for a healthy, romantic, love relationship between two adults who DO have choices and their love is not unconditional.

There are two parts to the love equation. That is all. And I always seemed to go for one or the other. Never both. Here they are in their simplest form:

First, I must love someone; respect them, care about them, be attracted to them, treat them well, be compatible with them and generally LIKE them, not fear intimacy or be emotionally closed off.

And secondly, they must love me; respect me, care about me, be attracted to me, treat me well, be compatible with me and generally LIKE me, not fear intimacy or be emotionally closed off.

The other thing I realized is that when we hold on to an addiction for so long, whatever that addiction may be (alcohol, drugs, cigarettes, the real or imagined love of another person, etc.) it is because it gives us a (false) sense of security. It makes us feel tethered, grounded, and whole. It takes the edge off of living.

When I divorced, I wrote in my journal that I felt, at the same time, happy to be free and extremely fearful. I felt like I was no longer connected to something bigger and greater than myself. I felt ALONE, ISOLATED and FREE-FLOATING. I didn't like that feeling. So within six months of being a newly divorced woman, I made two very bad choices: I started smoking cigarettes again (a habit I had quit for ten years) AND I latched on to a man who wasn't good for me but gave me that sense of being connected again.

When we are afraid and lonely and scared of the "emptiness" of life, we tend to make very bad choices. But what can we do to get over that fear? What can we do to stop the pain we feel when we are "floating around in space?"

An alcoholic will drink. An overeater will eat more. Someone who fears loneliness will cling to another person...

None of these things really takes the edge off. You take a "hit" of your drug of choice and it only causes the desire for another hit and another. Next thing you know, you're a junkie.

I realized that my "qualifier" did the same thing for me as cigarettes. I could lose my identity, not have to deal with my pain and suffering, and I could feel tethered to something bigger than myself as long as I had him around. He took the edge off. Just like alcohol to the drunk, drugs to the junkie, food to the overeater.

Addiction is born out of a need to feel connected. When you don't feel connected to anything, you suddenly want to put something into your body, eat something, smoke something, DO SOMETHING with someone. Westerners have equated a feeling of security and wholeness with the idea that something (food, drugs or another person) will fill the "void" and make you whole. Well, what if you started believing that THERE IS NO VOID? That you are complete.

This is how my recovery began. After years of reflection and self-discovery, I believe I now have the courage to face many of my fears. I believe I have made peace with myself. If someone doesn't like me, I let it all go. I have enough self-esteem in me now to say there are a million men in the world who will treat me with love and respect and because I believe in my own worth, I will hold out for something better.

I do not kick and scream and cry like a child if someone leaves me or "abandons" me. I know I will be ok and that I can survive on my own if I have to. I look in the mirror every day and say "not bad." I can deal with that. And most importantly, I no longer cling to a fantasy of meeting a perfect love because I now realize that is something that is made, not given.

It has not been an easy road. I equate recovery to mountain climbing. You struggle up the side of this huge mountain, hanging on for dear life, maybe slide down a time or two. But then you come to a place of rest and you sit back and look up to see how far you still have to go.

And you think nothing has changed and there are enormous lessons still to be learned, the summit is so far away...But then, you look down to see how far you've come and you realize the climbing, the struggling has brought you farther than you ever imagined!

I am Not Alone

I've probably been a love addict since my childhood. Since I've been working the Love Addicts Anonymous (LAA) program, I've had the opportunity to look back at my past relationships and see that I was addicted to all of them in one way or another. Today I'm not in a "love" relationship, I'm working on changing me and my core issues, so that if my Higher Power chooses to allow me to have another relationship, I will be healthy. I'm getting healthier. . . but it has taken a lot of work to get there.

It had been several months since K and I had broken up. It was my first relationship after my divorce. I had several years in another program and thought I was ready for another love. I gave myself totally to him, he told me he loved me, that he was super committed, and that I was beautiful. All those words melted my heart and I opened myself up. I'll give more detail on that later, but after a while, he got bored and let me go. I was absolutely devastated. I tried everything I could think of to get over it. Every day, every minute, I was thinking about K. I told my OA sponsor that I was thinking about him like this. She said, "R..., this is not love, this is obsession." Of course I was angered, but in that moment I broke down, streams of tears coming down my cheeks. I got on my knees and admitted that I didn't know how to love and that's when I got here.

My first love was M. It was a junior high relationship. I wanted to kiss but he didn't. I couldn't figure out why he didn't want to kiss. . . years later I found out he was gay. But even after we broke up and I was only 15 years old, I fantasized that we would get back together. I thought of him all the time. It took months for me to get over him and I was only 15.

Next came another M. He and I met in a theater group. He was nothing like me, however he showed me affection. I fell in love with almost anyone who showed me affection. M got a part in a movie and went to London, England to film. We had a long distance phone relationship and while he was there, decided he wasn't ready for a serious relationship. I was devastated again and couldn't get over it.

Next came W. W asked me to be his women after only one date. I accepted. Soon he said he wasn't sure he wanted to be with me. Instead of getting devastated, I broke up with him to protect myself.

Next came V. V and I married. We had nothing in common. He was a fantasy for me, and made me feel important. I was a rich girl, he was a poor, bad boy and it was just like the movies. . . sort of. He told me all I wanted to hear, but needed a green card to live legally here in the U.S. Afraid of being alone, I married him. It lasted 17 years, but I had three affairs in the midst. I even temporarily left V for a married man, thinking the married man would leave his wife and make me his own. That never happened. V and I had three kids. After our youngest turned 5, addictions took over and we divorced. It was very painful.

Next came J. J showed up at my door wanting to know if his daughter could have my daughter spend the night over at his house so she would have a friend to play with. He mentioned that he was a widower and I thought: "he's single." Go for it. And I invited him to a Valentine's party. He called me a few hours before the party and cancelled on me. Once in a while he would call or take me out, but he was more interested in my daughters than me....he may have molested one of them. She doesn't remember, as he spiked the punch at a party and my daughter woke up, confused. It has taken a year of therapy for her to work through it. I was "drunk" on him, and couldn't see the warning signs.

Next was K which was the most painful break up I endured. It was our break up that led me to LAA, and I started seeing my part and why I am addicted to love.

I learned here that I am not alone. I started working the 12 steps. I got to Step 4 and learned so much about my part. I didn't get the emotional support I needed from a man growing up. My dad is an alcoholic and very logical. I needed love and hugs and talks.

While my dad provided for my physical needs, he was incapable of meeting my emotional needs. I searched for them in other men. I never learned about compatibility. I watched movies and Hollywood educated me on how relationships work. I had and still have a lot of changes to make. I picked up a sponsor here. She gets me. We talk about once a week and talk about life, self esteem, and very intimate personal issues.

Today I am much healthier. I have done a lot of work on my self esteem and am not immediately falling for anyone who winks at me, calls me sweetheart, or shows me kindness. I am able to take a step back and watch. I am content being single. I would like to be in a loving relationship, but would rather be single, then in another sick relationship.

I have a long way to go, but am very grateful for this program.

A New Day

I was a nice, funny, intelligent, kind little girl and I was the wise eldest daughter of four children. I lived in a big beautiful, famous city and I attended the best Catholic school in town. My father had a very good job and we were well off. My parents were a beautiful couple. They were in love. And they were happy. We had a beautiful house, the right friends, the right cars, the right clothes, and the right accent.

Unfortunately something in this "perfect" life was not actually perfect. Our neighbor was a pedophile and it happened my parents trusted this man and often left my brothers and I in his care. From the time I was five years old until I was ten, I remember painful memories of this experience. I sensed something was wrong with him when I was eleven and I started avoiding him completely.

I had silent and hidden resentments towards him and unfortunately, also felt guilty. This horrible experience remained a secret for many years. I had the courage to talk about it only with my husband, for the first time when I was 23 and then later to therapists.

Another feature of this little girl was that she was "in love" with her father. He was so beautiful and so cool with his "Ray Ban" and his sports car (he was even a racer). He was a boss, he had power over so many people, he was always right, and everything he did was good and great and perfect. We children all adored him but we feared him also. He rarely beat us but he was extremely severe; he wanted us to stay silent when we had lunch together. He wanted us to behave impeccably.

Anyway I felt loved by my parents, especially my mother who was sweet and caring. I had and still have a beautiful relationship with her.

I had a turbulent adolescence. At 12, I experienced my first depression. Then I alternated periods of euphoria and periods of depression. (Now I know this is called bipolar disorder). When I was 15, I began using hash and I often got drunk. I had many love stories. I had crushes at the beginning and then, when I got my targets, I lost interest and found a way to leave the guy.

The first time I really fell in love, I was 18 and my boyfriend was 18 too. I walked on clouds and he was everything to me. It was the first time in my life I felt such sensations. It was high and limerence all the time. When he left me, I had a nervous breakdown. I lost sense of reality and recovered in a hospital for about 20 days. My parents and all the family moved from the big town to make me live in a quieter place in the countryside. I left the hospital and continued my therapy in the country house.

Slowly I came back into myself but a very deep depression started. I missed and regretted so much about my first love. I felt so bad. One night I attempted suicide. I cut my wrists. I was just 19. My father found me and saved my life. That was one of the worst days of my life.

When I was 23, I met my husband, a beautiful, intelligent, and good man. I felt I had found life for the first time. It was the first time after my 18 year old boyfriend that my heart beat that way again. I was in love! And this man was in love with me! A fairy tale. We got married after eight months and after another year my wonderful daughter was born.

Everything was perfect. But inside of me something was still broken and a happy family life was not enough to fix it. Sometimes I was depressed for months and I didn't know the reason. Sometimes I was euphoric and I didn't know the reason.
After the episode in my late teens, I didn't have any therapy and I didn't even know I needed it.

I didn't finish college. My father wanted me to work in his firm. I started working with so much enthusiasm. I wanted my daddy to be proud of his little girl. I hoped so much he would finally loved me, after years of absence of mind and unavailability. All this made my husband jealous and a sort of rivalry began between my father and my husband.

I worked for ten years with my father and in the end, I was 33 and I really didn't know who I was anymore. I felt exhausted. I felt like a loser who didn't have the courage to live her life but was living in the shadow of her father. I was tired. I wanted something else. I left my father's work and with my husband and my daughter, I moved to another town. I had to find a new job. I found a course to become an English interpreter and translator and I was selected. This course included a stage in a country of English language.

Guess what? During that stage I met my "Person of Attraction (Qualifier)." He was different. He was sweet. He made me feel like the most beautiful woman when he looked at me. Maybe he was the third greatest love of my life (but this is a very dramatic definition). He had everything to hook me. He reminded me of my father (he was cool). He was sweet. He was kind. He was strange. He was picturesque. He had a wonderful voice. He was beautiful. He was interested in me.

So the CRAZY DREAM started . . .

I started texting, phoning, emailing my Qualifier, who was overwhelmed from my behavior and didn't know what to do. He chose to not respond. How many tears this crazy dream cost me. I started fantasizing and obsessing in such a deep way that many times, I was not present in reality, but was lost in my world of dreams. One day I was so lost in my dreams that I started confusing reality with dreams and thoughts and I had to call my former psychiatrist. Finally I started my therapy for bipolar disorder and also took medications for psychosis. I went back to reality.

At this time, Pope John Paul II was dying. I started to pray. And I noticed that after praying, the obsession decreased. I started to pray every day. I found the strength to stop emailing my Qualifier. And only with prayer and willpower, could I control my addiction.

I went on like this for two years. I controlled my addiction. But my life seemed gray to me. I didn't know I was a Love Addict and I didn't know my life seemed gray to me because I missed the high of my addiction. One day I felt completely free from my "passion" (I still didn't know it was called addiction). I found my Qualifiers profile on social media and sent him a message, "just to say hello, don't worry, I'm just an old friend." I don't know why I sent that message, probably because my addiction was not healed yet. Anyway my Qualifier responded for the first time and he wanted to SEE me. Of course I wanted to meet him. So I met him and did what I thought I would never do: I was unfaithful to my husband…but the strength of addiction is so great.

After our meeting he said I was special and beautiful and great and so on, but this situation was really impossible and we had no future. But the addicted me went on in this way for two years, writing desperate emails to my Qualifier, but I never received an answer—heartache.

A pain that never ends. I didn't know a pain that never ends existed. It exists and it's called love addiction. Again, for the second time, I was dragged from my feelings to a place of a total weakness. I didn't find a solution to my pain and desperation; the more I called my Qualifier, the more he stayed silent.

One day I prayed so much, I asked God to make me find the solution inside of me, I wrote down this prayer and that day I found the LAA site. I felt like an outcast who has found an island. After six years of pain my insanity had a name: Love Addiction.

And there were others like me, others who had my same issues and others who were healed from this disease. This was the answer to my prayers.

When I joined the board and started posting and sharing with my new friends, fellow love addicts, I felt completely understood for the first time in my life. After so much pain, I felt a great joy. I was not alone anymore. The first thing I thought was that I had finally found a solution. I wanted to help others. I felt a great love for all people suffering from love addiction. So I became a "newcomers greeter."

After only two days, I was already working for the site that was saving my life. The power of the group is essential in helping us overcoming any kind of addiction. I was able to have "no contact" and stopped emailing my Qualifier (who never responded) and I posted on the board every time I felt the urge of contact.

"No contact" gave me back my dignity in about two months and it gave me clarity of mind. I no longer considered myself "the stalker." I was me again. Humiliations, frustrations, and confusion didn't hurt me anymore.

I started working the 12 Steps. I woke up at 4:00 in the morning and read the Big Book online. It was June 2009. Every word I read was a balm and gave me new hope that I could fight my addiction. I was sustained by my strong faith in God and I felt Him close to me. In working the steps, I was completely honest with myself for the first time in my life. I faced my past, my childhood, my abuse, my weakness, and my fears. It was a healing journey inside of me.

I had some slips during the healing process and they made me feel really bad, because now I knew that relapse behavior was insanity, it was wrong and not good for me. I had slips even in late recovery and they reminded me of the power of this addiction.

About two months ago, I read a very beautiful book called "Smile Across your Heart" by Laurie Martin. The book is about self love and it transformed my heart. I became able to feel the good energy of the Divine and I found a personal way to meditate. Meditation is like eating spiritual food; it nurtures our soul and it makes us feel whole, complete and happy.

My tools of Recovery are:

1. Talking to other members, asking and giving advice.

2. Working the 12 steps with honesty and perseverance.

3. Reading all the precious information and the experiences of others on the board.

4. Reading many, many books about love addiction because it's important to know our addiction. This helps us to know ourselves and to recognize how our behavior makes us feel. We can then find the tools to work on ourselves and fight our disease. Reading books about spirituality is also important to me.

5. Prayer, contact with the Divine, and dialogue with God. Find a way to pray and meditate, it will give you strength and peace.

6. Individual therapy.

7. Understanding we are powerless over this addiction, so we can only surrender to our Higher Power if we want to heal. We have to work, read, study, take action, and change.

8. We CAN change, change is possible (Read "The Art of Changing" by Susan Peabody). We have the power to change, which is the power of healing.

9. When we start feeling free from our addiction, we can start to know and celebrate ourselves. This is our prize.

Since that day, on May 2009, I have slowly retraced all of my past. I have finally understood what happened to me in the 70s, in that beautiful, famous city, when my parents were far away on one of their trips. And I've understood that I'm not crazy; I just have a bipolar disorder, due to the stress I suffered when I was a child. And that I have love addiction because I thought that a beautiful, mysterious stranger, who reminded me of my father, could save me, once and for all, from all the pain I suffered in my life.

Today, thanks to this board, Susan Peabody's books, and my LAA friends, I feel I'm healing… but I think I had to live through all of this. I had to be molested as a child, I had to find a Qualifier, and I had to suffer so much to finally find a way home.

I will always be grateful to LAA for saving my life.

Looking for Love

Growing up in my home was not always happy. I was traumatized at a very young age. My father was an alcoholic but functional. My mom she was just a teen herself. Fast forward, who would have known the damage that lay ahead. I was very reserved as a teen and in early adult life. I had attachment issues I am certain of. Most of my life I dealt with low self-esteem and sadness. I'm sure I was suffering from depression at a young age.

I longed to be wanted and I would fantasize about my "perfect prince." However, I also avoided close intimacy. I went through a series of failed relationships including two marriages and two divorces while on my quest. I craved the excitement and romance that the initial contact brought.

Once the romance went away or things started to get too close, I found myself on the next quest. While I was wrapped and consumed in looking for love and romance, my personal life suffered.

Dealing with the after effects of not only my love addiction but also my sex addiction brought great pain. I would quit jobs for a quest and thus my finances would be ruined. Everything in my life took a back seat including my family while on my quest for love.

My life became completely unmanageable. I looked for love in all the wrong places without ever loving myself. I discovered 12 step programs recently in life. I went through Overeaters Anonymous, Sexaholic Anonymous, Sex Addicts Anonymous, Emotions Anonymous, Sex and Love Addicts Anonymous.

However my life changed once I discovered Love Addicts Anonymous. I didn't have any local groups. I started out just reading Susan Peabody's *Addiction to Love*. I then began to read everything else I could find about love addiction. I remember thinking to myself that this addiction sounds a lot like me. I'm an 'Obsessed Love Addict' and a 'Codependent Love Addict' among many others upon my discovery. I was ready for recovery. I was home.

Free at Last

At first I didn't think my story was worth telling. I did not experience the trauma that so many of the people whose stories I have heard did. I grew up in a suburb of Ohio. There were six of us in my family: Mom, Dad, two brothers, a sister and me. I was the 2nd born. There was no alcohol use in our family and no drug use. My parents were faithful to one another (to the best of my knowledge) and although my parents talk of a few bouts of financial hardship when I was very young, I don't remember experiencing any poverty. We had a nice home in a nice neighborhood and I went to good schools. I had good friends and did not have health problems. There were routines, boundaries, and predictability in my life. I was not physically or sexually abused. There was nothing out of the ordinary in my upbringing—on the surface anyway.

Just recently, I had an emotional upset in my life and needed comfort. I reached out to my sponsor, my therapist, and a CODA friend. I was listened to, comforted, and shown love in many different ways. I experienced such an outpouring of caring that it stopped me in my tracks.

There were people who thought I was worthy of love and I knew it was genuine and unconditional. Then I thought back to my childhood. I was a shy child and quiet who sucked her thumb until she was six years old to soothe and comfort herself. I do not remember being comforted or hugged or told I was loved.

Children need physical connection, eye contact, verbal affirmations telling them that they are worthy. I did not receive enough of this. But I was a good kid, obedient and quiet. As a young child, I tried pleasing my parents to get their love and acceptance. I did well in school and loved reading; I started creating fantasies from the books I read as soon as I was old enough to read. I did not know it at the time but now know that I was creating fantasies to relieve the loneliness I felt. My inner world was one of emotional longing and I have always felt a gaping hole inside myself. And nothing ever filled that hole.

I began a dysfunctional relationship with food when I was very young. I remember coming home from elementary school and although my mom was a housewife and my dad worked at home, I do not remember being greeted by either parent. Instead I would raid the snack cupboard. I would eat these little snack cakes: several of them.

My mom would later question who was eating all the snacks but I was too ashamed to admit it was me. I was trying to fill up that empty hole. I have always felt hungry and have battled with bulimia and other forms of disordered eating for most of my life.

As I entered puberty, there was nothing I wanted more in the world than to have a boyfriend. And the songs, movies, and books I was exposed to encouraged this. This, I believed, was where I would find true happiness and someone to love me. I watched the other girls, more attractive than me, who wore lots of makeup and had parents who weren't as strict as mine. These were the girls the boys liked. But when I was 16, I met a boy who liked me! And I liked him!

We started dating and he was my first love and first sexual relationship. I discovered the high this love relationship gave me. I was ecstatically in love, could think of nothing besides him, reveled in how he kissed me and held me and told him he loved me. I had found paradise and that emptiness was finally satiated.

We were together for 18 months and although I had no comparison, I still remember that relationship as being good. Then one day he told me he wanted to date other girls; he was only 15 when we started dating and he had not dated others.

The pain caught me off guard: he was my lifeline and it was suddenly cut off. I thought I would die. I wanted to die. I was truly devastated in a way I did not know I could be. I didn't know human beings could hurt like this.

My parents were clueless about how to help me and they made me feel ashamed as if I should "get over it." Mostly we didn't even acknowledge that my world had just shattered. I had stopped contact with the few girlfriends I had when I started seeing my boyfriend and now they had gone off to college, gotten married or moved away. I was alone in my suffering and it was the most painful time of my life.

And so I began self medicating. I binged and purged. I starved myself. I cut myself before that sort of thing became well known. I tried overdosing on pills. I tried to commit suicide in various ways but I was really crying out for help.

I stalked my ex-boyfriend. I stalked his new girlfriend. One night resulted in my ex-boyfriend crashing his car with me in hot pursuit. I hid out in the fields behind his house and laid down in the tall grass one night and prayed that I would die. The police found me there the next morning. I just wanted to end the intolerable pain. Everyone thought I was crazy and I believed them. I knew my world was awful but had no name to put on it and did not know it could be any better. My life was not worth living.

By this time, my parents decided to move to Arizona with my younger brother and sister. I think they wanted to get away from me and my theatrics. My mom helped me find a job and a room to rent and they left. My attempts to harm myself intensified. In a frantic effort to survive, I made a conscious decision to transform myself so I could never be hurt in this way again. I thought women were the ones who suffered so much in breakups but not men. So I did a makeover of myself: I

changed my style of clothing to black leather
jackets and combat boots and I started cussing
profusely. I took up smoking. I started hanging out
with coworkers who went out drinking after
work—every night of the week.

Then I discovered the numbing effect of alcohol. I
was smoking pot and experimenting with speed and
depressants. My bulimia was out of control; I was
binging and purging daily—sometimes several
times a day. I started taking sexual risks. After
about a year of this, I visited my parents in Arizona
for Christmas. I left the freezing temperatures and
heavy snow of Ohio's snow belt and spent
Christmas in warm sunny Arizona with palm trees
and blue skies.

I knew I was on a downward spiral and made the
decision to quit my job and move from Ohio to
Arizona for a fresh start. The decision was made out
of my love addiction: I knew I could not continue
living the way I was and I needed to get away. I was
19 years old.

In Arizona, I realized that it was not easy to adjust
from living on my own to living with my parents.
They watched "The Waltons" at night and went to
bed by 9:00 p.m. I was 19 years old and wanted to
socialize and go out. Soon I met the man I was to
marry and my mom was very happy for me. He was
6 years older than I was and loved the outdoors. He
introduced me to the Arizona desert: we went

camping and hiking and fishing. He was looking for a roommate and I needed to get out of my parents' house so I moved in with him.

Things were not right from the start but I still had no reference point regarding relationships with men. He criticized me a lot and nothing I did was ever good enough. I kept trying to improve myself to get his approval and so he would be nice to me. We fought a lot and as things got worse, I knew this was not a relationship to stay in. I tried to leave and go back home.

This was the first time I had tried to leave a relationship that was not good for me and I found I could not do it. I remember lying on a bed at my parents' house feeling like I was dying. I did not understand what I was feeling and knew I had to go back to him to relieve the pain. So I did and this cycle continued. I married him and had four children.

I was married for 24 years to this man who was emotionally and verbally abusive. The kids and I "walked on eggshells." It was a living hell and although I tried numerous times, I could not leave him. My parents did not support divorce and did not offer any help. It was so painful to watch this highly volatile family life play out with my kids. I did all I could to protect them from the dysfunction but I did not leave this abusive man. I stayed. I tried to change my own behavior and that did not work. I

tried to stand up for myself and my kids and that
did not work.

I sank into hopeless depression again and again. I
sought counseling many times. I joined support
groups and exercise classes and tried to keep myself
alive so I could feed and nurture my kids in the
environment I had created for us. I learned ways to
cope with his raging and manipulating abuse. I
coped as best I could and yet the emotional and
verbal abuse took a high toll and I still bear those
scars. As do my kids. I did not protect them as a
parent should.

Yet somewhere in me there is a will to survive. I
had a friend who was in a similar marriage and she
started taking classes at the community college. She
suggested I try it out. I waited another year until my
twins started Kindergarten and then I signed up for
a class.

It took me a year of signing up and withdrawing
from class before I got the courage to set foot in
that classroom. My first class was psychology and
in the pages of the textbook, I saw my husband and
diagnosed him as having "borderline personality"
disorder. I had a name to my misery and I felt
validated. SOMETHING really was wrong!

My husband would not pay for my college classes
so I applied for and received a Pell Grant. I started

going to the community college part time and I loved it. I began to see that this was MY WAY OUT. It took me seven years to complete my education and I graduated with a Master's degree in Social Work and a 4.0 GPA with Honors when I was 47 years old. During those seven years, I latched onto this dream that I would be able to support myself and my kids and leave my husband. This is what kept me going as the abuse and dysfunction continued and escalated year after year. I had HOPE!

After graduation, I found my first job and during the employee physical exam, it was discovered that I had thyroid cancer. I believe this was a result of living under the extremely chaotic and dysfunctional family life. I needed my husband's health insurance for the medical treatment and so even though I had one foot out the door, I stayed once again. It took a year to get through the surgery and treatment and then I finally walked away—for good.

I divorced in 2004 and bought my own home. Three of my four kids came with me; my middle son, did not. During the last years of the marriage, he had become the rebellious teenager—acting out the family's pain. His father told him I was leaving the family because of him. I sought counseling for him and the family but as long as I was in the marriage, there was little chance of recovery or healing for anyone. I tried having him live with the rest of us but his behavior was unacceptable and I worried about the effect on my young teen daughters.

I was working full time outside of the home for the first time and leaving my kids home alone after school was a difficult adjustment for all of us. When he turned 18, I told my son he could not live with us anymore and he began trying to fend for himself. I carry the guilt to this day.

And so began my new life without abuse. I reveled in my new found peace and serenity. I was suddenly a career woman and a single mother. Life was good and I had about two years of healing and I experienced my own strength. As my kids grew up and needed me less, I starting feeling isolated; I did not have many friends or a social life.

Eventually, I joined a hiking club and began a lifelong love affair with the great outdoors. I also developed a crush on a man in the hiking club: he was a heavy drinker, very charming, fun, flirtatious, much older than me, and he had very different religious and political views than me. We never officially dated but this began my interest in men post divorce.

For the next 15 years, I went through a series of long term intimate relationships with men. After my abusive marriage of 24 years, I did not remarry. I dated four men over this time and each ended painfully. After each breakup, I felt like I was dying. With maturity, I thought I could handle a breakup better but this was not the case. Each ending was like that first breakup all over again. I had lost my lifeline and I could not heal from it.

The unresolved pain from my "first love" piled onto each subsequent breakup. The only way I could alleviate the intolerable pain was to start a new relationship. And I was in a lot of denial about what I was doing: I knew I was not ready for a new relationship so I would tell each new partner, exactly that. I would say "I'm not ready to date but just want a friend or just want a dance partner or to date casually."

I now know that with love addiction, these people were destined to become my next partners.

My last breakup was just over a year ago. I was with this man for two years and he was a good man; he had done his own recovery work years before. He treated me well. He was verbally and physically affectionate and he loved me. But my co-dependency and love addiction continued to create problems.

I had also developed a dance addiction by this time and this is how I was getting my validation from men: through the love relationships and the dancing (which I loved). I got into the relationship on the rebound and just needed someone to dance with. He quickly became my boyfriend. And my life soon became unmanageable. I could not end the relationship so I sabotaged it until he had to end it. This is when I realized that it's not about finding a "good man." I needed to get sober from relationships with men and take a hard look at what I was doing.

As in the past, the break up nearly killed me. I became so depressed I could not get out of bed to go to work. I found a therapist who said after six sessions, he would not work with me any further. My stomach was rolled in knots and I could not eat.

My obsessive thoughts about the breakup haunted me day and night and I could not sleep. I lost weight and applied for FML to keep my job. A coworker referred me to a therapist who was trained in co-dependency and addictions and I am forever grateful to him. This is where my recovery began and what would be a life-saving transformation.

I went into recovery kicking and screaming. I did not want to go to CODA groups and sit around and listen to "those people." I went anyway. After weeks of this, I told my therapist I was doing what he suggested but I was still suffering terribly. He asked if I shared (spoke) at the meetings and I said no. He suggested that I do this so back I went and unhappily shared. After a few weeks of this, I said again to my therapist, "I am sharing but still not feeling any better." He asked what time I arrived at the meetings and what time I left. This seemed like a no-brainer to me: I got there when the meeting started and left when it was over. He suggested I arrive 15 minutes early and stay 15 minutes afterwards. "What for?" I asked. He replied "to talk to people."

I rolled my eyes at him and then started arriving early and staying late and forcing myself to talk to people. My therapy continued in this way. Gently but persistently, he led me down a path of recovery. I began to learn what it means to take care of myself and to value myself enough to do so. I experimented with opening up and sharing my feelings with trustworthy people who were also in recovery. My sessions provided an opportunity to create a relationship with a man in the safe boundaries of a therapeutic environment. I started attending some of the CODA workshops and social events.

I began going to Sex and Love Addiction meetings. I found a sponsor and started working the 12 steps. I slowly started trusting and liking some of the women I was meeting and friendships formed. I called people when I needed support. I began exploring what spirituality means to me and added these teachings to my recovery. I learned about addiction and the names for what I was experiencing: cravings, acting out, withdrawal, triggers, bottom lines, staying sober, and I felt validated. I saw that I was not alone; there were other people who were going through similar experiences. I learned the tools of recovery and how they could work for me. One year after my last breakup, a CODA friend and I started a new Love Addicts Anonymous recovery group. There was a need for this recovery group and we saw how it benefitted us as well as others.

I recently celebrated a year and a half in recovery. I am grateful to each person who is helping me in my journey and for the 12 step recovery fellowship programs. My life is full and although I still have moments of sadness, I have more joy and gratitude than I have ever experienced in my life. I like who I am and I enjoy my own company. I also enjoy loving and intimate relationships with others in my life. Living without addiction has helped me to see that there is more to life than obsessively seeking pleasure to make myself feel good; my life gains meaning in being of service to others in need.

Conclusion

In closing, LAA would like to acknowledge that change is hard work. But you can do it. We hope your journey is both successful and worth all the effort. We know ours has been. We are not the people we were, we are the people we are going to be.

Reading List

Ackerman, Robert, and Susan Pickering. *Abused No More: Recovery for Women in Abusive and/or Codependent Alcoholic Relationships.* Blue Ridge Summit, PA: TAB Books, 1989.

Adams, Kenneth. *Silently Seduced: When Parents Make Their Children Partners – Understanding Covert Incest.* Deerfield Beach, Florida: Health Communications, 1992.

Appleton, William. *Fathers and Daughters.* Garden City, NY: Doubleday, 1981.

Ashner, Laurie. *When Parents Love Too Much: What Happens When Parents Won't Let Go.* New York, NY: Avon Books, 1991.

Aterburn, Stephen. *Addicted to Love: Recovery from Unhealthy Dependency in Love, Romantic Relationships and Sex.* Ann Arbor, MI: Servant Publications, 1991.

Bass, Ellen, and Laura Davis. *The Courage to Heal: A Guide for Women Surviving Child Sexual Abuse.* New York, NY: Harper and Row, 1988.

Beattie, Melody. *Codependent's Guide to the 12 Steps.* New York, NY: Prentice Hall, 1990.

Beattie, Melody. *Beyond Codependency and Getting Better All The Time.* San Francisco, CA: Harper/Hazelden, 1989.

Beattie, Melody. *Codependent No More: How to Stop Controlling Others and Start Caring For Yourself.* San Francisco, CA: Harper/Hazelden, 1987.

Berman, Steve. *The Six Demons of Love: Men's Fears of Intimacy.* New York, NY: McGraw-Hill, 1984.

Berne, Eric. *Games People Play: The Psychology of Human Relationships.* New York, NY: Grove Press, 1964.

Bireda, Martha. *Love Addiction: A Guide to Emotional Independence.* Oakland, CA: New Harbinger, 1990.

Bloomfield, Harold, and Leonard Felder. *Making Peace With Your Parents.* New York, NY: Ballantine Books, 1985.

Bradshaw, John: *Creating Love: The Next Great Stage in Growth.* New York, NY: Bantam Books, 1992.

Bradshaw, John. *Homecoming: Reclaiming and Championing Your Inner Child.* New York, NY: Bantam Books, 1990.

Bradshaw, John. *Healing The Shame That Binds You.* Deerfield Beach, Florida: Health Communications, Inc. 1988.

Bradshaw, John. *Bradshaw On The Family.* Deerfield Beach, Florida: Health Communications, Inc., 1988.

Branden, Nathaniel. *How to Raise Your Self-Esteem.* New York, NY: Bantam Books, 1987.

Branden, Nathaniel. *The Psychology of Romantic Love: Why Love Is, Why Love Is Born, Why It Sometimes Grows, Why It Sometimes Dies.* Los Angeles, CA: J.P. Tarcher, 1980.

Briggs, Dorothy. *Celebrate Yourself: Enhancing Your Own Self-Esteem.* Garden City, New York, NY: Doubleday, 1977.

Buges, Larry. *Love and Renewal: A Couple's Guide to Commitment.* Oakland, CA: New Harbinger Publications, 1990.

Burns, David. *Intimate Connection.* New York, NY: William Morrow, 1985.

Burns, David. *Feeling Good: The New Mood Therapy.* New York, NY: Morrow, 1980.

Butler, Pamela E. *Talking To Yourself.* San Francisco, CA: Harper and Row, 1983.

Carnes, Patrick. *Contrary to Love: Helping the Sexual Addict.* Minneapolis, Minnesota: CompCare Publishers, 1989.

Carnes, Patrick. *Out of the Shadows: Understanding Sexual Addiction.* Minneapolis: CompCare Publications, 1983.

Carter, Steven and Julia Sokul. *Men Who Can't Love: When a Man's Fear Makes Him Run From Commitment and What a Smart Woman Can Do About It.* New York, NY: M. Evans Co.; Berkeley Books, 1987.

Chopich, Erika and Margaret Paul. *Healing Your Aloneness: Finding Love and Wholeness Through Your Inner Child.* San Francisco, CA: Harper & Row, 1990.

Coates, Jennifer. *Women, Men & Language.* White Plains, NY: Longman, 1986.

Colgrove, Melba, Harold Bloomfield and Peter McWilliams. *How to Survive the Loss of a Love.* New York, NY: Bantam Books, 1976.

A Course in Miracles. Foundation For Inner Peace, 1975.

Covington, Stephanie. *Leaving the Enchanted Forest: The Path From Relationship Addiction.* San Francisco, CA: HarperSan Francisco, 1988.

Cowan, Connel, and Melvyn Kinder. *Women Men Love, Women Men Leave: What Makes Him Want to Commit.* New York, NY: Clarkson N. Potter, Inc., 1988.

Cowan, Connel, and Melvyn Kinder. *Smart Women, Foolish Choices: Finding the Right Man and Avoiding the Wrong Ones.* New York, NY: Clarkson N. Potter, 1985.

Cruse, Joseph: *Painful Affairs: Looking For Love Through Addiction and Codependency.* New York, NY: Doubleday, 1989.

Davidson, Joy. *The Agony of It All: The Drive For Drama and Excitement in Women's Lives.* New York, NY: Jeremy P. Tarcher, Inc., 1988.

Davis, Laura. *Allies in Healing.* New York, NY: Harper Perennial, 1991.

DeAngelis, Barbara: *Secrets About Men Every Woman Should Know.* New York, NY.

DeRoches, Brian. *Reclaiming Your Self: The Codependent's Recovery Plan.* New York, NY: Bantam Doubleday, 1990.

Diamond, Jed. *Looking For Love In All the Wrong Places: Overcoming Romantic and Sexual Addiction.* New York, NY: Putman, 1988.

Diamond, Jed. *Inside Out: Becoming My Own Man.* San Rafael, CA: Fifth Wave Press, 1983.

Dobson, James. *Love Must Be Tough.* (Christian literature) Word Books, 1983.

Dowling, Colette. *Cinderella Complex: Women's Hidden Fear of Independence.* New York, NY: Summit Books, 1981.

E. Blume, Sue. *Secret Survivors.* New York, NY: Wiley Books, 1990.

Evans, Patricia. *The Verbally Abusive Relationship.* Hobrook, Massachusetts: Bob Adams, Inc. 1992.

Fedders, Charlotte & Laura Elliot. New York, NY: Dell Books, 1988.

Firestone, Robert W., *The Fantasy Bond: Effects of Psychological Defenses on Interpersonal Relationships.* New York, NY.

Freedman, Rita. *Beauty Bound.* Lexington, Mass: Lexington Books, 1986.

Friedman, Sonya. *Men Are Just Desserts.* New York, NY: Warner Books, 1983.

Forward, Susan, and Craig Buck. *Obsessive Love: When Passion Holds You Prisoner.* New York, NY: Bantam Books, 1991.

Forward, Susan, and Crag Buck. *Toxic Parents.* New York, NY: Bantam Books, 1990.

Forward, Susan. *Men Who Hate Women and the Women Who Love Them.* New York, NY: Bantam Books, 1986.

Forward, Susan, and Craig Buck. *Betrayal of Innocence: Incest and Its Devastation.* Los Angeles, CA: Jeremy P. Tarcher (distributaed by St. Martin's Press), 1978.

Giler, Janet, and Kathleen Neumeyer. *Redefining Mr. Right.* Oakland, CA: New Harbinger Publications, 1992.

Gilett, Richard. *Change Your Mind, Change Your World.* New York, NY: Simon and Schuster, 1992

Goldberg, Herb. *The New Male Female Relationship.*

Gordon, Barbara. *I'm Dancing As Fast As I Can.* New York, NY: Harper and Row, 1979.

Gorski, Terence T. *The Players and Their Personalities: Understanding People Who Get Involved in Addictive Relationships.* Independence, MO: Herald House, 1989.

Gray, John. *Men Are From Mars and Women Are From Venus: A Practical Guide For Improving What You Want In Your Relationship.* New York, NY: Harper Collins, 1992.

Gray, John. *Men, Women and Relationships: Making Peace With the Opposite Sex.* Hillsboro, Oregon: Beyond Words Publishing, 1990.

Grizzle, Ann. *Mothers Who Love Too Much: Breaking Dependent Love Patterns in Family Relationships.* Westminister, MD: Ivy Books, 1991.

Halpern, Howard. *How to Break Your Addiction To a Person.* New York, NY: McGraw Hill, 1982.

Halpern, Howard. *Cutting Loose:* . New York, NY: Simon and Schuster, 1976.

Harris, Thomas. *I'm O.K., You're O.K.: A Practical Guide to Transactional Analysis.* New York.

Hauck, Paul. *Overcoming Frustration and Anger.* Philadelphia, PA: Westminister Press, 1974.

Hendrix, Harville. *Keeping the Love You Find.* New York, NY: Pocket Books, Simon & Schuster, 1992.

Hendrix, Harville. *Getting the Love You Want: A Guide For Couples.* New York, NY: Henry Holt & Company, 1988.

Hyde, Margaret. *Sexual Abuse, Let's Talk About It.* Philadelphia, PA: Westminister Press, 1984.

Imbach, Jeff: *The Recovery of Love: Christian Mysticism and the Addictive Society.* New York, NY: The Crossroad Publishing, 1991.

Jeffers, Susan. *Feel the Fear and Do It Anyway.* San Diego, CA: Harcourt, Brace, Jovanovich, 1987.

Johnson, Robert. *We: Understanding of the Psychology of Romantic Love.* San Francisco, CA: Harper and Row, 1983.

Johnson, Spencer. *One Minute For Myself.* New York, NY: William Morrow & Co., Inc., 1985.

Kasl, Charlotte D. *Women, Sex, and Addiction: The Search for Love and Power.* San Francisco, CA: HarperSan Francisco, 1990.

Kennedy, Eugene. *If You Really Knew Me Would You Still Like Me?* Minneapolis, MN: CompCare, 1983.

Keyes, Ken. *A Conscious Person's Guide to Relationships.* St. Mary, Kentucky: Living Love Publishers (distributed by Devores), 1979.

Kid, Sue Monk. *God's Joyful Surprise: Finding Yourself Loved.* (Christian literature) San Francisco, CA: Harper & Row, 1987.

Kierkegaard, Soren. *Works of Love,* translated by Howard and Edna Hong. (Christian literature) New York, NY: Harper and Row, 1962.

Kiley, Dan. *The Wendy Dilemma.* New York, NY: Arbor House Publishers, 1984.

Kiley, Dan. *The Peter Pan Syndrome.* New York, NY: Dodd & Mead, Co., 1983.

Kingma, Daphne Rose. *Coming Apart:.* New York, NY: Fawcett Crest, Ballantine Books, 1987.

Kreisman, Jerold and Hal Straus, *I Hate You, Don't Leave Me: Understanding the Borderline Personality*. Los Angeles, California: Price Stern Sloan, Inc., 1989.

Larsen, Earnie. *Stage II Relationships: Love Beyond Addiction*. New York, NY: Harper and Row, 1987.

Lee, John H. *I Don't Want To Be Alone: For Men and Women Who Want to Heal Addictive Relationships*. Deerfield Beach, FL: Health Communications, 1990.

Leman, Kevin. *The Pleasers: Women Who Can't Say "No" and the Men Who Control Them*. New York, NY: Dell Publishers, 1987.

Leonard, Linda. *The Wounded Woman: Healing the Father-Daughter Relationship*. Athens, Ohio: Swallow Press, 1982.

Lerner, H. *The Dance of Intimacy*. New York, NY: Harper and Row, 1989.

Lerner, H. *The Dance of Anger: A Woman's Guide to Changing the Patterns of Intimate Relationships*. New York, NY: Harper and Row, 1985.

Lorrance, Laslow. *Love Addict at Eighty-Four: Confessions of an Old Romantic.* New York, NY.

Love, Patricia. *The Emotional Incest Syndrome: What To Do When a Parent's Love Rules Your Life.* Bantam Books, 1990.

Ma, Anne Katherine. *Boundaries: Where You End and I Begin.* 205 West Touhy, Park Ridge, Illinois 60068, 1991.

Marlin, Emily. *Relationships in Recovery: Healing Strategies for Couples and Families.* New York, NY: Harper and Row, 1989.

May, Gerald, G. *Addiction and Grace: Love and Spirituality in the Healing of Addictions.* San Francisco, CA: HarperSan Francisco, 1991.

McKay, Matthew, and Peter Rogers, Joan Blades, Richard Gosse. *The Divorce Book.* Oakland, CA: New Harbinger Publications, 1984.

Mellody, Pia. *Facing Love Addiction: Giving Yourself the Power to Change the Way You Love.* San Francisco, CA: HarperSan Francisco, 1992.

Mellody, Pia. *Breaking Free: A Workbook for Facing Codependence.* San Francisco, CA: HarperSan Francisco, 1989.

Mellody, Pia. *Facing Codependence: What It Is, Where It Comes From and How It Sabotages Your Life.* San Francisco, CA: Harper.

Miller, Alice. *Drama of the Gifted Child.* New York, NY: Basic Books, 1981.

Miller, Joy. *My Holding You Up is Holding Me Back: Over Responsibility and Shame.* Deerfield Beach, Florida: Health Communications, 1991.

Miller, Joy. *Addictive Relationships: Reclaiming Your Boundaries.* Deerfield Beach, FL: Health Communications, 1989.

Missildine, W. Hugh. *Your Inner Child of the Past.* New York, NY: Simon & Schuster, 1963.

Moustakas, Clark. *Portraits of Loneliness and Love*: New York, NY: Prentice Hall, 1990.

Moustakas, Clark. *Loneliness and Love*: New York, NY: Prentice Hall, 1974.

Moustakas, Clark. *Loneliness.* New York, NY: Prentice Hall, 1961.

Nakken, Craig. *The Addictive Personality: Roots, Rituals and Recovery.* Center City, MN: Hazelden, 1988.

NiCarthy, Ginny. *Getting Free: A Handbook for Women in Abusive Relationships.* Seattle, Oregon: Seal Press, 1982.

Norwood, Robin. *Letters From Women Who Love Too Much: A Closer Look at Relationship Addiction and Recovery.* New York: NY Simon & Schuster, 1988.

Norwood, Robin. *Women Who Love Too Much: When You Keep Wishing and Hoping He'll Change.* New York, NY: Pocket Books, 1985.

Oliver-Diaz, Philip, and Patricia A. O'Gorman. *Twelve Steps to Self Parenting.* Deerfield Beach, Florida: Health Communications, 1988.

Paul, Jordan and Margaret Paul. *From Conflict to Caring.* Minneapolis, MN: CompCare Publishers, 1988.

Paul, Jordan, and Margaret Paul. *Do I have to Give Up Me to Be Loved By You?* Allen, Texas: Argus Communications, 1975.

Peabody, Susan. *Addiction to Love. The Art of Changing.* Random House, 1994.

Pearson, Carol. *The Hero Within.* San Francisco, CA: Harper and Row, 1986.

Peck, Scott. *The Road Less Traveled: A New Psychology of Love, Traditional Values, and Spiritual Growth.* New York, NY: Simon and Schuster, 1978.

Peele, Stanton. *Love and Addiction.* New York, NY: New American Library, 1975.

Person, Ethel, M. *Dreams of Love & Fateful Encounters.* (Mature love vs. romantic love) New York, NY: Viking-Penguin, 1989.

Peterson, Sylvia Ogden. *From Love That Hurts to Love That's Real (recovery workbook).* Park Ridge, Illinois Parkside Publishing Corporation, 1989.

Phelps, Janice Keller, and Alan E. Nourse. *The Hidden Addictions and How To Get Free.* New York, NY: Little, Brown, and Co, 1986.

Phillips, Debora with Robert Judd. *How to Fall Out of Love.* New York, NY: Warner Books, 1978.

Reynolds, David. *Playing Ball on Running Water.* New York, NY: William Morrow and Co., 1984.

Ricketson, Susan C. *Dilemma of Love: Healing Codependent Relationships at Different Stages of Life.* Deerfield Beach, FL: Health Communications, 1990.

Rosselini, Gayle, and Mark Worden. *Here Comes the Sun: Dealing With Depression.* Center City, MN: Hazelden, 1987.

Rosselini, Gayle, and Mark Worden. *Of Course You're Angry.* Center City, MN: Hazelden, 1985.

Rubin, Lillian. *Intimate Strangers.* New York, NY: Harper and Row, 1983.

Rubin, Theodore Isaac. *The Angry Book.* New York, NY: MacMillan, 1969.

Russianoff, Penelope. *Why Do I Think I'm Nothing Without a Man.* New York, NY: Bantam Books, 1982.

Sanford, Linda Tschirhart, and Mary Ellen Donovan. *Women and Self-Esteem.* New York, NY: Penguin Books, 1985.

Sandvig, Karen J. *Growing Out of An Alcoholic Family: Overcoming Addictive Patterns in*

Alcoholic Family Relationships. Ventura, CA: Regal, 1990.

Schaef, Ann. *Escape From Intimacy, Untangling the Love Addictions: Sex, Romance, Relationships.* San Francisco, CA: Harper and Row, 1989.

Schaef, Ann. *Co-Dependence: Misunderstood-Mistreated.* Minneapolis, MN: Winston Press, 1986.

Scarf, Maggie. *Intimate Partners: Patterns in Love and Marriage.* New York, NY: Random House, 1987.

Schaeffer, Brenda. *Is It Love, Or Is It Addiction?* Center City, MN: Hazelden, 1987.

Seabury, David. *The Art of Selfishness.* New York, NY: J. Messner, Inc. 1937.

Seixas, Judith and Geraldine Youcha. *Children of Alcoholism: A Survivors Manual.* New York, NY: Crown Publishers, 1985.

Shain, Merle. *When Lovers Are Friends.* Philadelphia, PA: Lippincott, 1978.

Sills, Judith. *Excess Baggage: Getting Out of Your Own Way; Overcoming the Blind Spots That*

Make Your Life Harder Than It Has to Be.
New York, NY: Viking Press, 1993.

Sills, Judith. *A Fine Romance: The Passage of
Courtship Meeting to Marriage.* New York,
NY: Ballantine Books, 1987.

Sills, Judith. *How to Stop Looking For Someone
Perfect and Find Someone to Love.* New York,
NY: Ballatine Books, 1984.

Smedes, James B. *Forgiving and Forgetting.* San
Francisco, CA: Harper and Row, 1984.

Smith, Manuel. *When I Say No I Feel Guilty.* Los
Angeles, CA: Pacifica Foundation, 1975.

Somers, Suzanne. *Keeping Secrets.* New York,
NY: Warner Books, 1988.

Tannen, Deborah. *You Just Don't Understand:
Women and Men in Conversation.* New York,
NY: Morrow, 1990.

Tannen, Deborah. *That's Not What I Mean: How
Conversational Style Makes or Breaks a
Relationship.* New York, NY: Ballantine
Books, 1986.

Taylor, Cathryn. *The Inner Child Workbook: What
to Do With Your Past When it Won't Go Away.*

Los Angeles, CA: Jeremy P. Tarcher, Perigee
Books, 1991.

Walker, Lenore. *The Battered Woman*. New York,
NY: Harper and Row, 1979.

Wakerman, Elyce. *Father Loss: Daughters Discuss
The Man That Got Away*. Garden City, NY:
Doubleday, 1984.

Wegscheider-Cruse, Sharon. *Coupleship: How to
Build a Relationship*. Deerfield Beach, Florida:
Health Communications, 1988.

Wegscheider-Cruse, Sharon. *Learning to Love
Yourself*. Deerfield Beach, Flordia: Health
Communications, Inc., 1987.

Wegscheider-Cruse, Sharon. *Choicemaking for Co-
dependents, Adult Children, and Spirituality
Seekers*. Pompano Beach, Florida: Health
Communications, Inc., 1985.

Weinhold, Barry. *Breaking Free of Addictive
Family Relationships*. Dallas, TX: Stillpoint,
1991.

Welwood, John. *Journey of the Heart: Intimate
Relationships and the Path of Love*. New
York, NY: Harper Perennial, 1991.

Welwood, John. *Challenge of the Heart: Love, Sex, & Intimacy In Changing Times.* Boston, MA: Shambhala Publications; New York, NY: Distributed in U.S. by Random House, 1985.

Whitfield, Charles. *Healing the Child Within: Discovery and Recovery For Adult Children of Dysfunctional Families.* Pompano Beach, Florida: Health Communications, 1987.

Wholey, Dennis. *Becoming Your Own Parent.* New York, NY: Doubleday, 1988.

Woititz, Janet. *Struggle For Intimacy.* Pompano Beach, Florida: Health Communications, 1985.

Woititz, Janet. *Adult Children of Alcoholics.* Pompano Beach, Florida: Health Communications, 1983.

Womack, William. *The Marriage Bed: Renewing Love, Friendship, Trust, and Romance.* Oakland, CA: New Harbinger Publications, 1991.

Wood, Barbara. *Children of Alcoholism: The Struggle For Self and Intimacy in Adult Life.*

Wright, H. Norman. *Making Peace With the Past.* (Christian literature) Old Tappan, New Jersey: H. Revell Co., 1985.

Zerof, Herbert. *Finding Intimacy: The Art of Happiness In Living Together*. New York, NY: Random House, 1978.

Disclaimer

The International Committee realizes that to some people a reading list is controversial. When our co-founder started her recovery, self-help books were banned from the fellowship hall where she got sober. However if her sponsor had not given her a copy of *Women Who Loves Too Much*, LAA would not exist today. We ask that you remain open minded about this.

If your favorite book is not here feel free to submit it to us.

Printed in Great Britain
by Amazon

26129339R00096